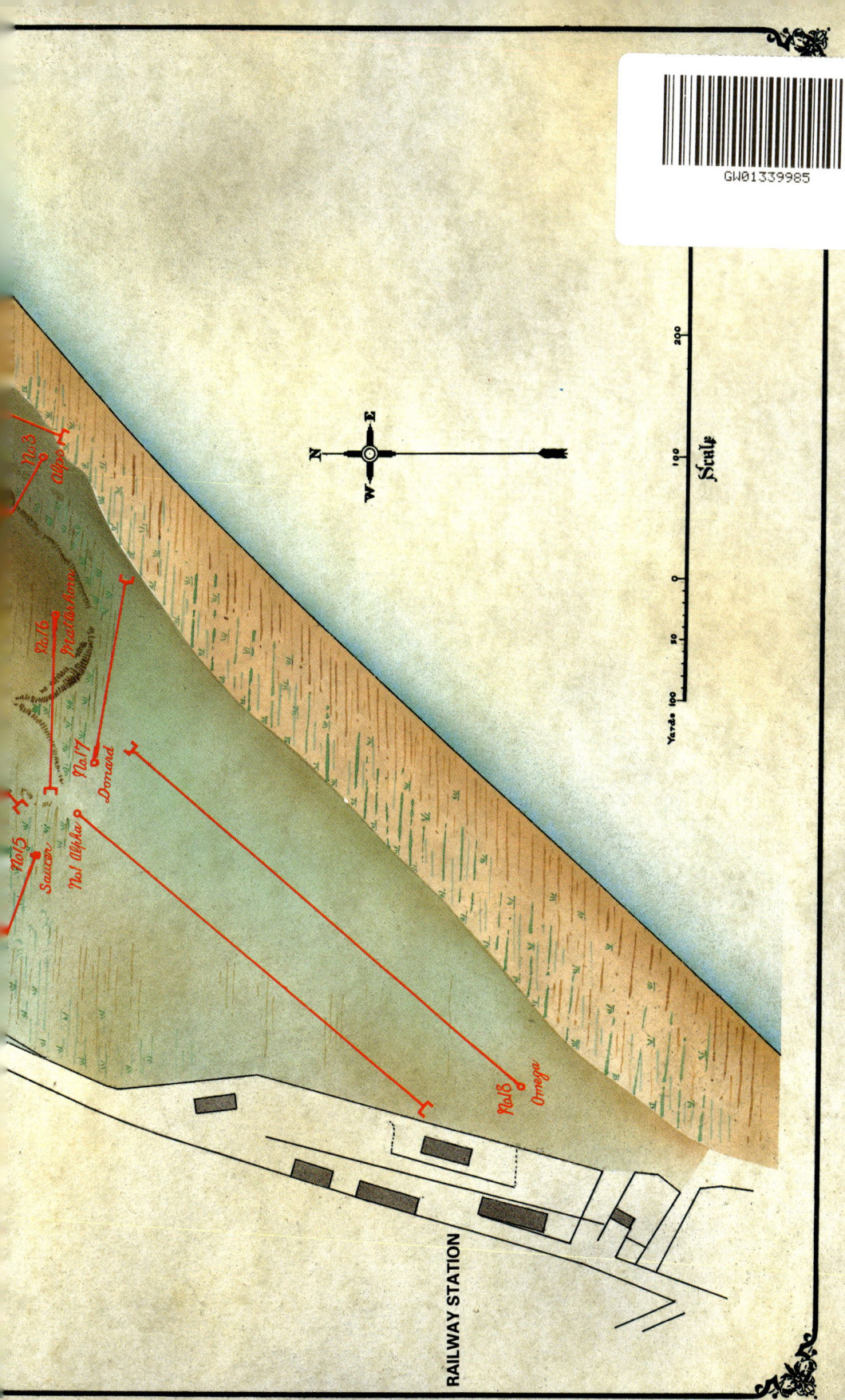

"The first known map of the links, probably circa 1892, and depicting what may well have been the original layout approved by Old Tom Morris."

RAILWAY STATION

ROYAL COUNTY DOWN
GOLF CLUB

THE FIRST CENTURY

© 1988 Harry McCaw and Brum Henderson

All rights reserved. This book, or any part thereof, may not be reproduced in any form without the written consent of the authors and publishers.

Published by The Royal County Down Golf Club
ISBN 0 9514430 0 3
Printed in Northern Ireland by
The Universities Press (Belfast) Limited.

ROYAL COUNTY DOWN GOLF CLUB

THE FIRST CENTURY

HARRY McCAW and BRUM HENDERSON

Acknowledgments

The authors acknowledge with gratitude much help and advice freely given from many quarters. In particular, they wish to record their thanks to:—

* Universities Press (Belfast) Ltd., who were represented by Mr. John Belshaw.
* Mr. Rowel Friers for his inimitable drawings
* Miss Doreen McDowell for dedicated hours typing innumerable drafts
* The Royal County Down Ladies Golf Club
* Mr. Alan Mackey of Ulster Television for photographic advice
* Mr. Isaac Smyth of Smyth's Photographic Services of Newcastle, Co. Down, for his admirable photographs of the course
* Mr. Bobby Burnet, Historian of the Royal and Ancient Golf Club of St. Andrews.

and lastly, but by no means least, the Henderson family for their great generosity (I.H.M.)

They also wish to thank each other. Work on this book has meant the renewal of a boyhood friendship, and the shared experience of stern debate on a mass of available material, and on the style to be adopted, were at times a test of sanity almost as great as that which can obtain on the course itself. Nevertheless, harmony prevailed, and it is their hope that this volume will provide something for everybody.

Contents

Page   1   From Warren to Links — Beginnings

Page 10   The Nineties — A Permanent Home

Page 25   Over the Hundred

Page 34   Edwardian Ladies

Page 46   War — And the Club Poet

Page 63   Straightness, Charm and the Lease

Page 74   The Prince, The Record and the Mourne

Page 86   Whiskey for Sale and an Airborne Kilt

Page 103   A "Character and Curtis Ladies

Page 111   Records, Rabbits and Re-birth

Page 124   Appendices

For this centenary memoire we have borrowed from the 1958 history written by James Henderson and updated in 1975 by Arthur Jones, then Secretary of the Club, but we have widened its scope to include unpublished and new material, photographs and illustrations. Inevitably, close study of minutes, record books and newspaper files, together with the prompting of personal memories, has unearthed so much that in the end our mission became one of selection and rejection. The apocryphal may mingle with the actual — as is the wont of golfers — but we have sought to portray the vigorous and richly diverse life of the Club during a century of profound changes in which golf remained — as ever — a test of perseverance and humility.

A majestic mountain backdrop; a five mile strand of golden sand; the "basket of eggs" of the small hills of County Down; and, above all, the northward prospect of fierce rough, whins in blossom, bracken, heather, narrow fairways, hungry bunkers and subtle greens — these views and the memories they evoke are etched in the minds of visitors and members, but there are others ... and we move back a century for them.

The new Club House
11th September, 1897

From Warren to Links — Beginnings

William Gibson's fascinating and scholarly researches in "Early Irish Golf" conclude irrefutably that the game, even in a primitive form, was played in Ireland at Bray in 1762, and that the Scottish Regiments garrisoned at the Curragh created a course of sorts there in the 1850s, but the pioneers of organised golf in Ireland were the seven signatories to a circular letter sent out on November 5th 1881 calling a meeting on November 9th to be held in the Chamber of Commerce, Belfast. These were G. L. Baillie, J. O. Brown, W. F. Collier, C. K. Cordner, J. Findlater, W. Murphy-Grimshaw, and Thomas Sinclair.

The prime mover was Sinclair who had seen golf played in St. Andrews that summer and, on return to Belfast, made exhaustive enquiries to find kindred spirits who might possess some knowledge of the game. These revealed that Dr. Collier, Headmaster of the Belfast Royal Academy, was acquainted with it. Even more encouraging, he had on his teaching staff one G. L. Baillie, a native of Musselburgh, who had actually played the game.

Sinclair and Baillie began prospecting for sites and their choice fell finally on the Kinnegar, Holywood. Others thought to be interested were informed, and in due course the Mayor (Sir Edward Porter Cowan), whose residence many years later became the home of the Royal Belfast Club, presided over a meeting of 18 men in the Belfast Chamber of Commerce. On the motion of Mr. Sinclair,

Dr. Collier and G. L. Baillie.

seconded by William Quartus Ewart (later Sir William) it was decided to form the Belfast Golf Club. Sinclair was elected the first Captain, Baillie the Honorary Secretary, and J. O. Brown the Honorary Treasurer. Fourteen of those present at this first meeting were formed into a committee and thus organised golf in Ireland began.

During the '80s the Belfast, Curragh, Dublin, Portrush, Aughnacloy, and Queen's County Heath Clubs came into existence, and to celebrate his year as Captain of the Belfast Club James Henderson had presented an all-Ireland Challenge Cup. Golf, therefore, was beginning to develop in Ireland and it was inevitable that some of the Belfast golfers whose families spent summer holidays at Newcastle would look over the stretch of sand-dunes known as The Warren at the County Down resort and see its great golfing potential.

Hugh, 5th Earl Annesley, first President of the Club.

A number of them summoned a meeting at Newcastle early in 1889 and Dr. Collier, one of the signatories to the original 1881 circular, proposed that "The County Down Golf Club should be formed". James Henderson (later Sir James Henderson, DL) immediate past Captain of the Belfast Club, proposed the election of G. L. Baillie as Honorary Secretary and Treasurer, and the 50 people who had agreed to be original members formed the first provisional committee. Thus was born the highly democratic but possibly unwieldy parent of the present, much smaller, Council. Even a committee of 50 did not appear to daunt the golfers of those days.

An extract from the minutes of this inaugural meeting on March 23, 1889, records that

"A meeting of those favourable to the establishment of golf at Newcastle was held today in the Hall of Mr. Lawrence's Dining Rooms, Newcastle. Lord Annesley presided and over 70 ladies and gentlemen were present."

The "Belfast Newsletter" of March 26, 1889 gives a detailed account and stated that immediately its first President, Lord Annesley, opened the meeting he ordered an adjournment to the links for the first competition.

£5 to start   Some sort of course, therefore, must have existed to have been played on that day, so who laid it out and where did it lie? The answers to both questions are shrouded in mystery but it does seem clear that G. L. Baillie of the Belfast Club was instrumental in laying out the first holes for the January 1889 minutes of that Club authorized him a sum not exceeding £5, followed two months later by a further £5, towards preliminary expenses. It is fair to assume that because neither the Slieve Donard Hotel nor Club House had been built the first course, a nine hole one, may have had its first tee somewhere near what is now Golf Links Road. Baillie's knowledge and advice were clearly invaluable, but he had not arrived on totally uncharted territory for the evidence is that golf in even a primitive form was being played there the previous year. George Combe, replying to the toast of the Club at the inaugural dinner for the new Club House some eight years later, said that "July 1888 had seen Mr. Gregg with a few of his friends playing over land which promised to be a golf course." He went on to say that the course was now mainly taken up by "the new hotel" which supports the thinking that the first tee was indeed not far away from the Station. "Later", he said, "Mr. Herdman and Mr. McGeagh went still further afield, and

"The Hill of Pisgah".

after mounting a hill called The Hill of Pisgah looked out over what appeared to them to be perfect golfing ground. That land was now occupied by the 15th and 16th holes" (in 1897). It is likely that the Hill of Pisgah, so named because from the Heights of Pisgah Moses had looked over the Promised Land, was the present 9th or 11th hill.

The Golfing Annual of 1889–90 described the course as being 9-holes with short and springy turf, hazards for the most part of the bunker and sandhill type, and greens in excellent order for a new links. It went on to say that

> *"a more beautiful situation for a golf course could scarcely be conceived, running as it does for over a mile along the shore of Dundrum Bay and back again".*

It mentions a 40 ft. high sandhill called The Matterhorn (and named this for many years), so it is reasonable to assume that the original 9-hole links lay on part of the present first nine holes.

The Matterhorn — but where did it lie?

Provisional Committee

The first meeting of the provisional committee was held on June 1, 1889. Dr. Collier presided and 11 others were present. They appointed a Council composed of names prominent in the life of Northern Ireland for generations:—

Thomas Andrews, R. Fetherston, Henry Gregg, James Henderson, Henry Herdman, Hugh C. Kelly, W. H. Smiles, C. E. Stronge and W. F. Thompson, with power to add "four local men" to their number. G. L. Baillie and Colonel Ross shouldered the duties of Honorary Secretary and Honorary Treasurer and a momentous decision was taken, namely to "employ Tom Morris of St. Andrews to lay out the course at an expense not to exceed £4". This was presumably to comment on the existing nine and make suggestions for a second.

Immediately after the meeting a competition was played in which Mr. Thomas Gilroy, Captain of the Dublin Golf Club "did an actual 98", it being noted by the "Newsletter" that

"it will probably be a long time before his record for the second round will be beaten. It only totalled 43, made up of

5 3 4 4 5 4 6 6 6 = 43"

Mr. Gilroy was clearly a doughty performer, playing off a handicap of plus 6 and finishing sixth. It was evidently inappropriate in those days to award a gross prize.

Four times Champion Golfer and then in his sixties, Morris visited the Club on Tuesday and Wednesday, July 16 and 17, 1889, and also played a match with Alex Day, professional. The Council recorded later, somewhat casually, that he had made "some valuable suggestions for the laying out of an 18 hole course."

The first official meeting of Council, elected in June 1889, was scheduled for July 15 but it collapsed for want of a quorum, and eventually re-assembled eight months later with five present — Henderson, Baillie, Fullerton, Herdman and Thompson. J. H. Moore-Garrett, agent of the Annesley Estate, had been invited to become the first Captain, but had declined, and Amar Lowry-Corry accepted the honour of being both the first Captain and Vice-President.

"Old Tom Morris" who laid out the links "for a sum not to exceed £4".
Reproduced by kind permission of The Royal and Ancient Golf Club of St. Andrews.

On April 20, 1890, the first annual meeting took place, preceded by a stroke competition over two rounds (it was still, therefore, a 9-hole course). A Belfast newspaper stated that:

"a ballot for partners having taken place, a start was made at the first teeing ground at 2 o'clock before a crowd of onlookers, many of whom were ladies. The greens were in fine order and high scoring was attributable to the great length of the holes, several over a quarter of a mile each, and to the great abundance of rabbit scrapes throughout the ground.

Scores reached the late 90s, even among the leaders. One gentleman registered 138".

Doubtless morale was restored by the 'hot soup and vegetables and cold viands' served in Lawrence's Dining Rooms beside the railway.

The handicap prize on the day was won by A. S. Matier (117-31 = 86), thus becoming the first holder of the Lowry-Corry Cup.

The same newspaper, continuing its report on the first A.G.M., recorded that one of the most notable events of the year had been the visit of Tom Morris, who had spent 2 days "on the ground" and had pronounced the links at Newcastle capable of being made into "one of the finest greens in the Kingdom". It was to be a long but interesting course and the Council were gradually clearing the ground expecting to have it ready for July 12 when they planned a two-day tournament which would, in all probability, "bring out some of the best known amateurs on the Scotch and English greens".

Some original members, with Lord and Lady Annesley in rear of picture.

The speed at which both nines were built and brought into play is fascinating proof that the course was carved from what already existed; and so it remains today — one of the great natural links of the world.

First 18 holes On June 25, 1889, the "Newsletter" recorded that by the following Saturday "the first 18 holes will be laid down at Newcastle" and the 1887 Amateur Champion, Horace G. Hutchinson, would visit Newcastle together with other well-known players from England and Scotland. He returned a 76 off plus 5. Two days later the new 18 holes were officially opened to members, Thomas Gilroy again having the best gross with 81

The original links and some of the less expert players complaining that many of the holes were too long and that at least three of them would have to be reduced to half their length. Their position is obscure, but a recently discovered map (c.1892) reproduced at the front of the book is almost certainly the original links on which Old Tom Morris advised. By 1894 extensive alterations had taken place, the results of which were described in the 1895/6 Golf Annual by H. M. Rush of Tantallon Golf Club:-

The "First" hole (283 yards) presents no great difficulty, but the lies from the tee are not good and the second shot will certainly be played off short heather; but careful play with the iron will take you home and the hole ought certainly to be a 4.

In playing the second or "Corner" hole (211 yards) a dead straight line must be kept for a pulled drive will be badly punished in the bent grass and rabbit scrapes that await it, whilst a heeled ball will get a stoney lie. The average driver should find himself just short of the green and a short pitch over the bunker or bank which guard the green will give a safe 4 and a possible 3.

And now we face the first of those bunkers which a writer in "Golf" has truly called "stupendous". The tee for the "Alps" (233 yards) is in the centre of an arena surrounded on all sides by towering sandhills. Right in front, and at a distance of 100 yards from the tee, stretches a terrible bunker. There is no playing round it; you must take your trusty club in hand and go for it; and who shall describe the feelings of that player who gets away a "bonnie lick" as he stands and watches his ball rise straight over the guide-post and fall out of sight beyond. Crossing the "Alps" by the steps the ball is seen lying on beautiful turf at the foot of the sandhills, and a pretty approach shot just strong enough to carry some sandy knolls will trickle down into the bowl-like putting-green sometimes used, which was laid out at an enormous expense; but the other green certainly improves the character of the hole. The fourth, or "Macormac's" hole (320 yards) requires a straight drive and an accurate approach, for one too weak is trapped badly whilst one too strong is apt to run over the green into sandy ground beyond.

We require all our nerve for the drive to the fifth, or "South Down" hole (316 yards); again a gaping bunker, 150 yards from the tee must be faced, but a strong straight drive will find a good lie in the valley between two huge sandy pits which wait with open mouths to swallow the unsteady driver's ball. The second shot requires judgment and you will probably do best to play short to the edge of another high bunker which guards the undulating green beyond. It is very difficult to get one's pitch to stay on the green, which is certainly a curious one and is known as the "Switch-back" green.

The sixth, or "St. John's Point" hole (280 yards) is one of the most difficult. The best line is slightly to the left. The green lies to the right of the course on raised ground between two sandhills and is also guarded by a trap bunker.

At this point the course turns and we play back along the other side of the valley which we have already traversed. Straight must be your drive for the seventh or "Donard" hole (430 yards) for broken ground lies to the left and ferns and heather to the right. A good straight second with the brassy or cleek should carry you beyond all danger of bunkers but the green is difficult to reach in 2 as a high mound guards it in front and undulating ground to the right and left. You may be content with a 5.

The ninth hole, or the "Pitch" (96 yards) requires great accuracy as the player who is not up will find himself in one of those pit-like sand bunkers so characteristic of the links, whilst the ground to the right and left is rough. It is safer to be too strong and be content with 4, though undoubtedly it is quite possible to hole out in 3, or even 2.

The Field Hole (15th) sited on what is presumably the present 18th.

The last hole out, "Magill's" (314 yards), is somewhat rough all through which is due to the fact that it is quite a recent addition. The drive requires to be straight as to the left and right lie hollows filled with bracken. A good cleek shot should take you home in 2 but, owing to the roughness of the ground, the ball gets little or no run and a third shot is often necessary to get within putting distance so that anyone who holes out in 5 may be quite content. This makes our score 41 for the outward journey — not brilliant golf but very good play for one who keeps it up for the round.

The tenth or "Deception" (340 yards) is a capital golfing hole. A good clean drive rather to the left is necessary as there is a lot of very rough ground in front of the tee. For the second a very accurate iron or cleek shot is required as the green lies in a hollow with fern-covered banks all round. The green is one of the finest on the course and the hole should certainly be a 5.

We next face the "Chasm" (225 yards) an excellent name for this difficult hole. A long, low straight drive should leave an iron pitch to the green and the steady putter will certainly be down in 4.

In driving to the twelfth, or "Ward's" hole (248 yards), we encounter the only water hazard on the course which confronts us in the nature of a pond. The short driver will not find any difficulty in playing round it, though the average driver will certainly go for it and find himself lying in grass which is rather heavy and consequently the approach shot requires care as to strength, but 4 is certainly par play.

The drive to the "Railway" hole (297 yards) is an awkward one as the railway runs right alongside and a heeled drive pays the penalty of a lost ball and distance. The grass through the green is decidedly heavy and the second shot requires great care as the sloping green is guarded by a nasty turf-dyke and bunker but there should be no difficulty in getting home in 3 and holing out in 5.

The "Punch Bowl" (476 yards) is very sporting. The lies are fairly good up to the bowl-shaped hollow from which this hole takes its name and the turf-dykes ensure that each shot shall be well struck. Three good long drives are required to get near the green and 6 for the hole may be considered good enough.

If a good drive is struck for the fifteenth, or "Field" hole (332 yards) the second should certainly be on the green which is a very fine one and two more should see you down.

The "Saucer" (440 yards) is a long hole and requires accurate line. Three good strokes should leave you on the green from the shape of which the hole is evidently named, and two more should be sufficient.

The "Matterhorn" (160 yards) looks very simple but how many good scores did I see spoilt there.

The "Home" hole (356 yards) presents no serious difficulty but as the lies are rather heavy it will probably require 3 to reach the green and 5 may be considered par play for the hole.

No plan of this course exists, which is a pity, but it is an intriguing exercise to imagine, from the foregoing descriptions, where the holes actually lay.

The Home Green, sited approximately where the Slieve Donard Hotel now stands.

Mr. Rush goes on to mention two "inventions" of George Combe:

"They were the teeing grounds invented and patented, and the little iron caps inside the holes which caught the ball and kept it from being covered with sand on a wet day. The teeing grounds were really a capital invention and were placed beside natural ones to give the golfer a choice. The object of them is to save the ordinary ground during very wet weather and to ensure a firm foothold. They are made of wood which is fixed firmly in the ground whilst in the centre is placed either a rough mat or piece of smooth rubber on which the ball is teed and at either end is a square of rough rubber which grips the boot well and prevents slipping."

The Nineties — a Permanent Home

In the '90s proper administration of the Club began, and in 1890 the first professional was appointed for the summer at 17s.6d a week. His name is recorded, simply, as Day, but he was probably a brother of the professional at Carnalea. Council instructed that "he devote his sole attention to the greens and not do any club repairing or making, and any person wishing to play with him should pay the Club a fee and not give him remuneration unless they wished."

Rabbit holes and scrapes

The first greenkeeper was also employed at 10s.0d a week, and Col. R. H. Wallace, one of the joint Honorary Secretaries, was instructed to enter into negotiations with Lord Annesley to secure a lease of The Warren "with the right to fill up rabbit holes and scrapes". Some months later he reported that expectations were promising but he did not realise negotiations would be so protracted for it was not until 1895 that a 25 year lease from Lord Annesley was ready for signature. It allowed the Club "the right to trap rabbits, fill up their holes and scrapes and make any alterations necessary to improve the ground for golfing purposes."

The same year it was recorded that the Belfast Club gave the County Down club £5 in return for the privilege of playing their links on the third Saturday every month "during the season". Bulk buying — but not ungenerous.

The first "giant" in the life of the Club began to emerge — George Combe. Educated at Rugby, he had his first golf tuition from Jack Burns at Warwick in 1888, and went on to be one of Ireland's finest players. An excellent all-round sportsman, he

The Combe Cup

George Combe.

had a powerful influence on all aspects of the Club affairs for many years and indeed on golf in Ireland. One of the first plus handicap golfers in the country, he was an eager founder of the Golfing Union of Ireland and held the office of Honorary Secretary from its formation until 1899. He worked indefatigably, years in advance of most, in the layout, upkeep and administration of golf courses, and also on rules and handicapping. He was the originator of a handicapping scheme used by the G.U.I., a great deal of which was adopted a long time later at the famous York Conference of British Golf Unions. In 1900 he prepared a "code of rules of golf" based on that promulgated by the R. & A. in 1892, but with amendments specially designed for Newcastle. Nevertheless, in 1903 the fate of Combe's rules was sealed and the Council felt it appropriate to adopt the new code approved by the R. & A. in 1902.

The Kelly Cup

The Combe Cup, given back to the Club in the 1960's by his family, is a fitting reminder of one of the founding fathers, as indeed is the Kelly Cup, traditionally played for on Easter Monday, and commemorating another great early pillar of golf at Newcastle and in Ireland. Hugh C. Kelly was Honorary Treasurer of the G.U.I. from 1891-1912, President from 1926 to 1929 and thereafter Honorary Life President until his death in 1945. In his time he was probably one of Ulster's greatest sportsmen; not only was he a gifted golfer but also an international at rugby and lacrosse, a keen huntsman and expert sailor, taking part in several Americas Cup races.

H. C. Kelly.

A Kithogue

A third great contributor to the Club in the early days was Dr. Magill. An original member, he was a resident of Newcastle and a man greatly respected by the whole community and by his patients. He was a member of Council, more or less continuously, until well into the 1920's, but his principal work was on the House Committee and as Honorary Secretary. His family were notable golfers, his son Robert winning the Irish Close Championship at the age of 17 when still a schoolboy. "Golf" magazine, in October 1891, stated that "this promising young player, who is a Kithogue, is likely to falsify the old golfing idiom that there cannot be a good left-handed player". Dr. Magill's daughter was a

Dr. Magill of Newcastle.   *Miss Magill — Irish Ladies Champion.*

power in Ladies golf over a long period, winning the Irish Ladies title in 1898 and runner up in 1897 and 1910.

Puzzled Perth

The Club, therefore, was making a significant impact on golf in Ireland, with many first class players and championship winners. It also led in its contribution to the game's legislation and organisation of championships, accepting the St. Andrews Code of Rules in 1892, subscribing to the purchase of a Close Championship Cup, instrumental in an original handicapping scheme, and arranging one of the first cross-channel inter-club matches in 1892 with the King James VI Club of Perth, one of the oldest golfing institutions in the world.

The match was a fifteen-a-side affair, County Down winning by 35 holes to 19. The gentlemen of the King James VI Club were an adventurous band, for this was their third trip to Ireland, the first being in April 1884 when they played the first cross-channel match ever played in Ireland, and against the Belfast club at Kinnegar. These were the very early days of the first course in the country and conditions were still primitive.

> "The holes greatly puzzled the Perth players because of their unusual and difficult character, and the primitive accessories to the game also interested them in a way. Of house accommodation on the course or near it there was none, and those gentlemen who journeyed with anything in addition to their golfing suits handed it over in faith to an individual in attendance. A tunnel dug in a sandhill with a door between two uprights did duty as a hotel and a place of safety for spare clubs. As for the caddies, they were provincial Irish of a most pronounced type, and voluble to a degree."

On a more mundane note, it is recorded that in 1891 Lawrence's Dining Rooms offered a lunch of cold meat, potatoes, bread and butter and cheese for 1s.6d. Bread, butter and cheese cost 6 pence, pastry 6 pence, and a dinner of soup or fish, joint, sweet and cheese was 2s.6d.

Thirst could be assuaged with whiskey at 6 pence a glass and stout or aerated water for 3 pence a bottle.

Buried in the Council minutes is a first brief mention of a second course, although no Ladies Club officially existed until 1894, and on which a caddie fee would be 4 pence. There is no record of where this lay, or of how many holes it consisted, but it may be assumed that it covered land somewhere around the existing opening and closing holes on No. 2 course. Rather than any major schemes, it seems clear that both courses gradually evolved, many of the changes not even being recorded. For instance, in the December 1891 edition of *"Golf"* the following (although not noted in Council records) appears:-

> "It has been arranged to extend the present course by bringing in some excellent golfing ground along the sea from the present fourth green, which will provide three new sporting holes and enable some of the zig-zags on the railway side to be done away with. A new green is being laid down for the Alps hole and the Matterhorn and Corner greens enlarged".

First Ladies' Council 1894.
(L to R) Miss L. Brush, Hon. Treas.; Miss N. Graham; Miss MacLaine; Mrs. J. W. Hodges, Capt.; Miss M. Tyrrell; Miss Tyrrell, Hon. Sec.

First Green Committee

The first Green Committee was formed in 1891 and, with the House Committee, was instructed by Council to complete the furnishing of the Club premises and erect a notice-board at the first teeing ground "embodying a few of the important rules".

Some of the members were clearly not too well acquainted with the rules for, early in 1893, the winner of the Captain's Prize had been announced and published in the newspapers when a member wrote to the Council some days later claiming that he had had a better score than any of those published. He had forgotten to return his card so the Council made short work of him. Even better was the member who was told in September 1893 to return the cup he had won in November 1891 because it had been discovered (a shade belatedly!) that he had paid neither his entrance fee nor subscription at the time.

Dr. Magill was clearly in charge of House matters but it is not clear to whom the newly appointed greenkeeper reported, although annual reports in the minutes gave credit to John MacCormac (who took his seat on Council in 1892 and after whom the third hole was named) for his care of the links.

While the Club was growing in numbers its expenses were increasing fast and Council decreed a levy of 6 pence per member per round "to pay off the debt of the Club".

"... had paid neither entrance fee nor subscription".

The Ladies Club was formalised in 1894 with Countess Annesley as its first President and its members were given permission to play on "the long course" every day except Saturdays and competition days.

Professional perks

Towards the end of the same year the Club decided to stop selling golf balls and to allow the professional "to have this business as a perquisite". A few months later the erection of a shop for him was authorised. The greenkeeper sought "£150 per annum to continue his contract" but Council, clearly thinking that it was not unreasonable but perhaps considering that a straightforward agreement was infra dig, offered him £2.10.0d a week with a bonus of £10 each half year.

The first Steward, Robert Garrod, was appointed "custodian of the Clubhouse" in March 1895 at £52 per annum. He was held in high esteem by the members and his family also appeared to be employed en bloc, evidenced by the Christmas Fund details of 1900.

Christmas Fund 1900.

From the earliest days of the railway,

Newcastle had become a popular holiday resort. In 1896, David Strain, the first manager of the Ulster Bank's Carlisle Circus branch, wrote to his directors asking permission to stay with his family in the town during the month of August. In the reply which he received, agreeing to his request, the following warning was appended:— "Be cautious of the golfing fraternity, where a large number of them very needy, and many of them are habitual drinkers". Many years later Stanley Ferguson recalled that his father had been acquainted with the director concerned, describing him as "a benevolent old gentleman, but hardly a man of the world."

CLUB HOUSE.

During 1895 it was decided to build a club house in place of the accommodation provided by the Belfast and County Down Railway on the platform. The original structure, subsequently enlarged, was designed by Vincent Craig, brother of the first Viscount Craigavon, and completed in two years at a cost of £2,200. Such goods and chattels as could be used were transferred from the old "club house" and new items ordered.

"Needles and showers"

The inauguration of the building was celebrated on September 11, 1897 and part of the "Belfast Newsletter's" description of it reads:—

"The style of the structure bears strong resemblance to old English ... A staircase off the corridor which leads to the dining room then runs to the basement where there are large and well fitted dressing rooms, lavatories and baths, including needle and showers. A smaller apartment contains a stove and this will prove useful for the drying of members' clothes in rainy weather. Ample accommodation is provided for bicycles."

A banquet was held in the evening at which more than 300 members and some specially invited guests were present, but its preparation and presentation must have been beyond the capabilities of Sergeant Garrod and his family, so the services of Everest, the steward of the Royal Belfast Club were secured. The Council of the day, all present, comprised the President, Earl Annesley, Vice-Presidents Lord Arthur Hill MP and Major R. H. Wallace, P. T. Truesdale, W. J. MacGeagh, Henry Herdman, John MacCormac, Henry Gregg, H. J. Johnston, Ernest Young, George S. Clark, George Combe and Fred Hoey. The Honorary Secretary was Colonel H. D. Cutbill and the Honorary Treasurer Claude Brownlow JP.

List of furniture from old Club House (1897). *List of new furniture from Hanna & Browne 1897.*

The "Newsletter" reported the dinner in great detail and continued:—

Colonel James M'Calmont, M.P., not only well known as a golfer but also in many other sports, said that they could not but congratulate themselves on the wonderful vitality that existed in the golf clubs in Ulster. It could not be said that they were living in the flower of their youth, but he thought the opening of that Clubhouse that day would at least prove that golfing in Ireland had arrived at the very heyday of its prosperity.

Mr. Thomas Andrews toasted "Prosperity to the County Down Golf Club". It was perhaps not unfitting that that toast should be proposed by a railway man, because the interests of both were inseparably bound up. (Applause). He could have wished, however, that that toast had been allotted to someone better acquainted than he was with the mysteries of the royal game of golf — someone better able to do justice to the toast. ("No, no"). He, unfortunately, was wholly ignorant of "brasseys" and "drivers" and, would they believe it, until recently he was under the impression that "the Matterhorn" was in Switzerland. (Laughter). One thing they all knew — that that golf club possessed links which were second to none in the kingdom. (Applause)."

In 1898 another "giant" who was to dominate the affairs of the club for many years became Captain — Fred Hoey. His tenure of office was followed by his election as Honorary Secretary, a post which he held for a total of 21 years during which his genial presence and bustling efficiency involved him in practically every facet of the club's life and only terminated when he was re-called to serve as Captain once more in 1923. His year of office was an eventful one and the minutes show continuous course improvements.

Co. Down Golf Club.
INAUGURAL DINNER
at opening of the
NEW CLUB HOUSE
NEWCASTLE.
CO DOWN.

11th September 1897.

MENU.

A NINE HOLE MATCH.

AMONTILLADO.

HARE SOUP.
"One up and Eight to play."

TURBOT AND LOBSTER SAUCE.
"Well played, partner."

DUMINY,
1884.

ROAST CHICKENS.
"Like as they lie."

YORK HAM.
"Dead Sty-mied."

ST. ESTÈPHE.
1875.

SIRLOIN OF BEEF.
"Hazard a slice."

GROUSE.
"A Foul Shot."

COCKBURN'S
PORT,
1878.

APPLE PIE.
STEWED PLUMS.
"Play it with a spoon."

CHEESE AND CELERY.
"Dormy one."

DESSERT.
"Gobbled the Hole, and all even."

PLAY IT AGAIN SOME DAY.

Menu of Inaugural Dinner
to mark the opening of the new club house in 1897.

Castlewellan Castle, the home of the Annesley family.

The rolling foothills of the Mourne Mountains.

In August some problems were being encountered with the green staff and the Honorary Secretary was instructed

> "to intimate to Laird (the greenkeeper) that the Council expected the following hours of labour for his men shall be strictly adhered to viz from 7.00 a.m. to 6.00 p.m. with one hour for dinner, or from 6.00 a.m. to 6.00 p.m. with one hour for breakfast and one hour for dinner".

Par and bogey scores of "the green" were assimilated at this time (so the term par is not a recent invention) and the aggregate of these became 80 — out in 39 and back in 41.

Fred Hoey.

In September a decision was taken to hold what was probably the club's first mixed foursome. The ladies were invited to use the clubhouse on what must have been a successful day, at least in the eyes of one lady competitor who, whether in admiration of her partner's golf or his person, extended a written proposal of marriage on the back of the programme. No repetition of this is recorded of subsequent mixed foursomes competitions.

Leap Year
Dear Sir,
   Being informed by a Lady friend much older than myself that it was the custom when she was young to make use of the prevailing leap year I now take the opportunity it offers & I beg very serious attention to a few words. In the first place I have to request that after due consideration you will return an answer speaking in true sentiments from your heart, without reserve. You must be aware that I have a great regard & love for you, How far yours extends remains to be proved. I am no

20

longer a giddy young girl but fully capable of fullfilling the duties of a wife trusting there is a husband to be found. Ask yourself a few questions from your heart and if perfectly satisfied perhaps you will accept the challenge remembering as before observed that it is leap year when Ladies "Pop the question" as they did in ancient days. If I am wrong let the matter rest you keep your council and I'll keep mine and if no answer upon the subject I suppose I shall be at liberty to "Pop the question elsewhere.
Believe me, Dear Sir, in all sincerity,
           "Yours if you please".

The Professionals come

In October that year the Club held its first major professional event and provided prize money of 100 guineas. With the exception of James Braid and Willie Park, all the leading professionals of the day took part, including Vardon, Taylor, Sayers, Herd, Kirkaldy and Fernie. Vardon beat Taylor by 12 and 11 in a somewhat one-sided final but broke the course record in the process, lowering it by three shots to 71 in the morning round. Interviewed after the event he declared "he had never in all his life played such a game as he did today", adding that it was hard on Taylor, after playing so well, to be beaten so badly.

The Green Staff — circa 1900.

The social life of the club was never forgotten, even during the winter months. Earlier in the year in March, following a Saturday competition, it was reported that the golfers who had participated during the day

> *"dined at Mr. Lawrence's, the clubhouse being handed over to Mr. Woodhouse in preparation for his cinematograph exhibition. After dinner, which was served in excellent style, an adjournment was made to the clubhouse and a very successful entertainment was carried through. During the evening Messrs. McCleery, Caughey, Gunning and Bill contributed songs, which were admirably sung, and exceedingly well received. Mr. Woodside's exhibition of the Lumiere Cinematograph was carried through in his well-known artistic style, and all of the scenes were heartily applauded, the "Turnout of the Belfast Fire Brigade" "A Cockfight", and "The Capture of a Wild Horse by a Lassoo" being especially appreciated. At 11.00 p.m. the members of the club returned to Belfast in a special train which the County Down Railway Company had courteously placed at their disposal."*

Won with 101   A good account of severe conditions is found in the "Newsletter" of 1898 when an 18 hole scratch medal, the Figgis Challenge Cup, was played for on December 27:—

> "The entry was rather small owing to the furious gale and as Newcastle is not a green which can be negotiated in a gale with a wooden putter (as Hoylake and some other greens can) the scoring ruled high — that is to say, high on paper, but to those who were down at Newcastle to witness the play it was a matter of wonder that a round could be made at all. More than once players were on a green in two or three strokes, and took eight or ten more to hole out, their ball being blown hither and thither in the most ridiculous fashion, and the greens were so keen and in such splendid condition that this liveliness on the part of the 'guttas' was very much accentuated". The winner returned a gross 101 with only 8 finishing.

Elections and appointments proved interesting and notable were some who were to contribute signally to the life of the club in later years such as Fred Rogers and C. S. Harden. Viscount Glerawly, son and heir of the 5th Earl Annesley, was elected an Honorary Member although only 15 years old. He was a talented golfer, winning the South of Ireland championship in 1906 and contesting the final of The Close against Lionel Munn in 1914. He had succeeded to the title by that time but, sadly, was killed in a flying accident in the 1914-1918 war. He was a great loss to the club of which he had become President and indeed to Irish golf. C. S. Harden, while he was putting the new Malone course

May Hezlet.

into shape, was appointed "curator" of the County Down links and was the first to perceive the perennial menace of coastal erosion.

That Spring saw the Irish Ladies Championship being won by Miss May Hezlet of the famous Portrush golfing family. Newspaper reports of the time tended to wax lyrical and the "Newsletter" was no exception. An 1899 report shows a classic golfing "purple passage":—

> *"If the actual opening of the Irish Ladies Golf Championship Tournament at Newcastle lacked the accessory of brilliant sunshine, simple amends were made by the atmospheric deities when the contest proper was inaugurated. The weather was worthy of the merrie month, in that mood which poets loved to dwell upon, when the maypole and the morris dance were better known than the royal game which Scotland has taught half the world to love. Competitors and their friends were guests of the gentlemen members. The massive championship bowl was flanked by its memento miniature, and with a gold medal for the lady champion, a silver pin-box for the runner-up, handsome silver baskets for the semi-finalists and consolation prizes material in substance and value."*

Reporters of the day were not completely male chauvinists for they extolled *"A promising player in Miss M. Hezlet who won her round by grand play, and her performance admittedly a revelation to many of the gentlemen golfers. Apt as a rule to speak somewhat patronisingly of what can be done by golfers of that sex proverbially known as 'the weaker', they in this instance candidly questioned the ability of most among their own number to surpass or even to equal this splendid round."*

The year 1899 also saw a dispute with one of the caddies, resulting in strict rules, but for many years dinners were held in the club at which the caddies were waited on by the members. Nevertheless, they went on strike in 1901 but this was resolved with a modest fee increase and a happy tradition of mutual respect took root. Caddies in those days who were prepared to attend Newcastle Technical School had their fees paid by the club.

". . . resolved with a modest fee increase".

And so the 1800s closed with a young, lively club contributing vitally to the game in Ireland, and with its members demonstrating enormous zeal and mixed talent.

Advertisements.

C. S. BUTCHART, Golf Specialist.

A few of the Courses planned, constructed, and advised on:—

ANTRIM
BANGOR
BAD KISSENGEN
BUNDORAN
BELVOIR PARK
BLEAKDOWN
FORTWILLIAM
HIGHGATE
HUNSTANTON
LANKE
NORTH MIDDLESEX
OBERGLOGAU
PORTER'S PARK
ROYAL CO. DOWN
WEST HILL
WHITEHEAD
WORPLESDON

C. S. BUTCHART, *Professional to the Berlin Golf Club.*

MAKER OF THE WORLD'S MOST FAMOUS CLUBS.

Golf Courses laid out, constructed and reported upon. Inclusive Estimates submitted. Golf Links Grass Seeds supplied for all situations and conditions of soil. Prices and terms on application.

ADDRESS—
BERLIN GOLF CLUB, SPANDAUER CHAUSSEE, WEST END bei BERLIN.

Over the Hundred

A new century dawned and the Club had, in common with many other institutions born in the Victorian era, set its standards and laid its foundations with care and vision.

George Combe's guidance is clearly evident. The Council gave the Green Committee (Combe!) "power to make arrangements for the future management of the green" and within days he outlined proposals which included terminating the green-keeper's employment and giving Butchart an extra 5 shillings a week to pay for an extra two or, if need be, three men for the course who would be better supervised and "under the intelligent guidance of a practical golfer". He also outlined course improvements to be carried out that winter, this time recorded in the Minutes. They must have been quite significant and the first real major alteration. For instance:—

"5th hole — See to setting back of tee
6th hole — Set back 6th tee sixty yards thus making hole 3 good shots.
8th hole — Set back 9th tee 50 yards making it 2 good shots
11th hole — Lengthen Dundrum 60 yards and make it 3 good shots."

... and there were, in fact, alterations at 16 of the 18 holes.

C. S. Butchart had been engaged the previous year as professional, club maker, and caddie master, at a wage of 15/-d a week, with a penny commission on caddies. He must have been a remarkable man for not only did he appear to carry out the duties of caddie master and course supervisor but also in the four years he remained in the Club's employment established a lucrative club-making business and created a factory within corrugated iron buildings lying between the Club House and tenth tee from which hundreds of clubs were sent all over the world.

He also taught some young Newcastle men (including the brothers Kidd) to be club-makers and they in turn went to other courses such as the Old Malone when it was at Stranmillis before the first world war. In those days, of course, there were no steel shafts and he imported timber "in the rough" from America. An interesting contemporary account described how the timber was cut into blocks and stored "allowing about an inch per year for seasoning before it could be used". This was the first instance of machine made clubs in Ireland, which by then had become quite common in England and Scotland, and together with his ball-making and re-covering operations in the same building he employed some 20 people. His clubs were highly prized and those who own them today are in possession of collectors' pieces. He resigned in September 1904 and the Club bought his workshop for £30. Seymour Dunn was appointed professional and club-maker, with charge of caddies, and two years later Alex Robertson became professional, a position he held for many years.

Bustling Balfour   The year 1900 saw George Balfour, Chief Secretary for Ireland, visiting the course for a remarkably rapid day off politics. To facilitate his visit the County Down Railway placed a special train at his disposal and

> *"upon being left by his host, Lord Londonderry, at Newtownards Station at 10.00 a.m. (presumably he was staying at Mount Stewart) Newcastle was reached within the hour. The Chief Secretary showed excellent form, making very few mistakes, and his driving and putting were recorded as being 'especially good'."*

The Irish Open Amateur tradition had begun in the 1890's but when it came to County Down for the third time in 1900 the holder, the legendary John Ball, was unable to compete as he was serving in the Boer War. He had by that time been Amateur Champion five times, a feat only equalled by Michael Bonallack at Newcastle 70 years later.

Golf reporting was full, meticulous and elegant and "The Scotsman" wrote of part of Harold Hilton's final against S. H. Fry of Royal Mid-Surrey:—

> *"From the tee Mr. Fry had a heavy lie and he seemingly erred in judgment. He might have reached the green with the cleek. He took the brassey, duffed the stroke, was afterwards very wide with the iron, and completely ruined his chance of a half. Down in a perfect 4, Mr. Hilton gained the lead which, however, he lost at South Down, a very sporting hole, not owing to his being trapped, but owing to his opponent's superior play on the green. Approaching the fifth Mr. Hilton handled the iron in indifferent fashion. He was wide, and was punished in sandy bents to the right of the green. Strong is his recovery, he had never the ghost of a chance of a half, the hole going to Mr. Fry in a par 4. At Donard he lost his lead because he was not on the green in his second, while Mr. Hilton was home with a beautiful brassey stroke, and was down in 4."*

Harold Hilton.

The match, however, was a one-sided affair and Hilton, in a near faultless display, won by 11 and 9 in the 36 hole match.

In 1901 Council Minutes were typed for the first time, a welcome improvement on the

26

scratchy black calligraphy of the first 12 years, although this was occasionally enriched by pure copperplate. It was a volunteer's typewriter for even in 1908 Council rejected as "unnecessary" the purchase of a permanent one.

Early in 1901 the Club Steward died. The Minutes record "The Council are desirous of placing on record the great loss the Club has sustained in the death of Quarter Master Sergeant Garrod, a most efficient and trustworthy steward". He was clearly a stern old warrior for the local newspaper described what must have been a very large funeral attended by the members and people of Newcastle which

> "took place from the Club House after a short but impressive service therein conducted by the Rector. The coffin, covered by the Union Jack, was borne to the new burial ground at Tullybrannigan where the remains of the good old soldier, who had fought his last fight, were laid to rest under the flag of his country."

Pawky Foursome Players

Many of the newspaper accounts of those days were detailed and lyrical. Of the Easter Meeting in 1901 the "Northern Whig" reported:—

> *"It was one of the most brilliant and successful golf tournaments ever held there, and fell no whit behind the traditional esprit in the manner in which the latest great reunion was celebrated. The weather conditions were all that could be desired, the wind serving to accustom players to the sudden rise in temperature and occasionally merely deflecting ineptly-driven tee shots. The large number of English and Scottish visitors did the hotels and lodging-houses a good turn, and from Good Friday to the moment of writing not a bed can be found for love or money.*
>
> *None but parlour golfers could have found fault with the meteorological conditions. A couple of showers in the early morning freshened up the course and imparted to the putting greens that keeness which delights the heart of the inspired putter. What Mr. Arthur Balfour has described as the acme of golfing bliss — "a tolerable day, a tolerant green, and a tolerable opponent" — obtained and everything went without a hitch from morn till dewy eve. The hum of industry pervaded the recesses of Butchart's commodious new workshop and showrooms, and the precincts of the first tee and the last green swarmed with golfers, old and young, ex-champions and embryo champions and pawky old foursome players, some of the latter inclined to embonpoint, and some "whose hose, well saved, a world too wide for their shrunk shank" — practising putts and approaches with a determination to play in strict accordance with accepted theories and win if possible. It was very pleasing to all County Down golfers that the first prize should be won by two English players, so many of whom are at present patronising the magnificent green."*

"... the hum of industry pervaded the recesses of Butchart's commodious new workshop".

Later in the summer of 1902 the Council "approved of getting a horse and new mowing machine" and one of the members, while practising, drove through the upper door of the Club House. It was recorded that "the ball cannoned off the inside of the door on to the door of the reading room, which room it entered, breaking nothing."

In that year the scratch was 80. Winning scores had been four and five strokes above this and Council noted that handicaps were not to be cut unless a player showed promise, that they were not to exceed 18, and those over 9 would compete for medals among themselves.

"...which room it entered, breaking nothing"

The Autumn Meeting of 1902 marked the culmination of two or three years significant work on the course begun in the winter of 1900 under George Combe's single minded and probably autocratic guidance. It is the first time that the course is recorded as being in two loops with "the ninth and eighteenth greens on either side of the Club House, advantages which will be apparent to golfers without enumeration."

The changes, few of which are actually recorded, involved making several new holes and interchanging others, with the result that only six of the original holes were left, the other twelve being in some way varied.

A detailed contemporary description of the new layout does exist, and the result of Combe's labours could not have been very different from the first of two maps printed at the back of the book. The changes were quite significant and are clearly seen in a comparison of the lengths of holes on the old and new courses.

Hole	Old Course	New Course	Hole	Old Course	New Course
1	200 yds	550 yds	10	215 yds	200 yds
2	195 yds	320 yds	11	320 yds	250 yds
3	300 yds	280 yds	12	400 yds	360 yds
4	320 yds	340 yds	13	235 yds	200 yds
5	280 yds	350 yds	14	500 yds	340 yds
6	360 yds	360 yds	15	330 yds	560 yds
7	95 yds	140 yds	16	465 yds	330 yds
8	306 yds	320 yds	17	175 yds	220 yds
9	245 yds	200 yds	18	210 yds	380 yds

This Autumn Meeting of 1902 concluded with an exhibition match between James Braid and Sandy Herd, the then ex-champion and champion golfer respectively.

"Braid used a Springvale ball and Herd took the Haskell, while a large and fashionable crowd watched them play for a purse of sovereigns."

Jingoistic reader

After the match, in which Herd gave a masterly display to win by 4 and 2, the "Northern Whig" wrote a spirited leading article, clearly enraged that the golfing powers-that-be of the day had not yet seen fit to bring a major British Championship to Ireland:—

"It will be remembered that in May of last year a deputation was sent from this country to wait on the Committee which is entrusted with the fixing of the venue for the Amateur Championship. The committee treated our delegates with scant courtesy and declined to receive them. This year our petition in favour of holding a championship meeting in Ireland was heard, but peremptorily refused. The august body which treated our claims so unfavourably consists of representatives from the most important golf clubs in the world — the Royal and Ancient, the Honourable Company of Edinburgh Golfers, the Royal Liverpool, the St. George's and Prestwick. The position of these clubs could not be gainsaid but it may be permitted to us to dispute the justice of the verdict their representatives arrived at — that there is no suitable green in this country for deciding the blue riband of the game; that there is no championship course in Ireland.

It is possible that these gentlemen would modify their adverse opinion if they had been at Newcastle on Saturday and it is probable that if they put Herd and Braid, open champion and ex-champion, into the witness-box, the evidence for the petitioners would go far to upset the previous decision. There is a championship course at Newcastle now 5,760 yards long, with five miles more to take in on the shore of Dundrum Bay if so much be required...."

Mordantly, it continued:—

"While awaiting the realisation of this dismal forecast we might be going on with the extension of the Newcastle course from the first tee to St. John's Point, providing a ferry at Dundrum. The truth is that the present course at Newcastle has as long a range, as fine greens, and as noble hazards as the keenest golfer could desire, and the splendid scenery of the Mourne range is more to be desired than the flat lands of St. Andrews or the morass of Muirfield."

Whether or not this stinging literary contribution was ever read by those who ruled the game is not recorded. Perhaps it was, for the Amateur Championship did not come to Newcastle for another 68 years!

"stand over"

During the winter of 1903 Combe was clearly unhappy about some of the alterations for which he had been responsible and he asked permission to make further changes, mainly to the length of the 11th, 12th, and 13th holes. Council agreed to his request but cautiously stipulated that £100 expenditure was not to be exceeded. They also rejected the idea that the Club should have a legal adviser and evolved a

The "Golfers' Express"

masterly phrase (often repeated later) regarding potentially awkward matters that "it be allowed to stand over to the next meeting".

In the Spring of 1904 Fred Heyn, who had been negotiating on behalf of the Club, reached an agreement with the County Down Railway

Waiting to board the "Golfers Express" (c 1935)

Company in which the latter undertook to place two trains at the Club's disposal free of charge to members every Saturday, the 10.10 a.m. from Belfast and the 5.35 p.m. from Newcastle in the evening. The Club would also receive £100 per annum and, in return, visitors resident in the Hotel would be entitled to play on the links at half price. This was the first mention of what became the Golfers' Express which ran for many years thereafter with a special coach fitted with comfortable chairs and tables. The coach itself, which had begun life in 1897 as the Royal Saloon, was for the rest of its days used solely by the golfing fraternity and travelled next to the engine on the 12 Noon express from Queen's Quay Station every Saturday. For the rest of the week it lay under cover in the station.

Much keenly contested bridge was played, one member losing a rubber before the train left Belfast. On the return journey the train was backed up a siding at Ballynahinch and while "up the cut", as it was termed, stakes were doubled. Every Saturday the Caddy Master met the train and all clubs were taken to the Clubhouse on handcarts.

Two lines

Two years later, in 1906, the Great Northern Railway opened their link line from Ballyroney to Newcastle, thus allowing golfers to approach by rail from two directions, but before this event one of the club members came every Saturday from Banbridge to Ballyroney with his bicycle in the guard's van, pedalling the remainder of the journey.

"... *an unusually high number of holes in one*".

He also carried with him a small stone jar full of whiskey, usually finished by the time he reached Newcastle. He seldom played golf, but when the weather was even reasonably good he sat by the ninth green (now the putting green) and in those days a single shot blind hole. His impish sense of humour, accentuated by the contents of the stone jar, was some years later reputed to have accounted for the unusually high number of recorded holes in one at the ninth.

When the train was eventually discontinued a golfers 'bus was initiated. Bridge could be played upstairs but with little comfort, the player on one of the outside seats being frequently unseated due to sudden changes of direction. After a short time the 'bus was taken off and, although sporadic attempts were made over the years to resume the service, it was never really a success except during petrol rationing.

An indication of golf's growing popularity was evidenced by an early request from the Grain and Farm Trade Golf Club to use the links. This was possibly the first Society to be allowed its use.

An imposing entry in the Minutes of October 1906 records that "a letter was read from Vice Admiral William May thanking Council for placing the links at the disposal of the Atlantic Fleet".

And why not!

Part of the old town of Newcastle.

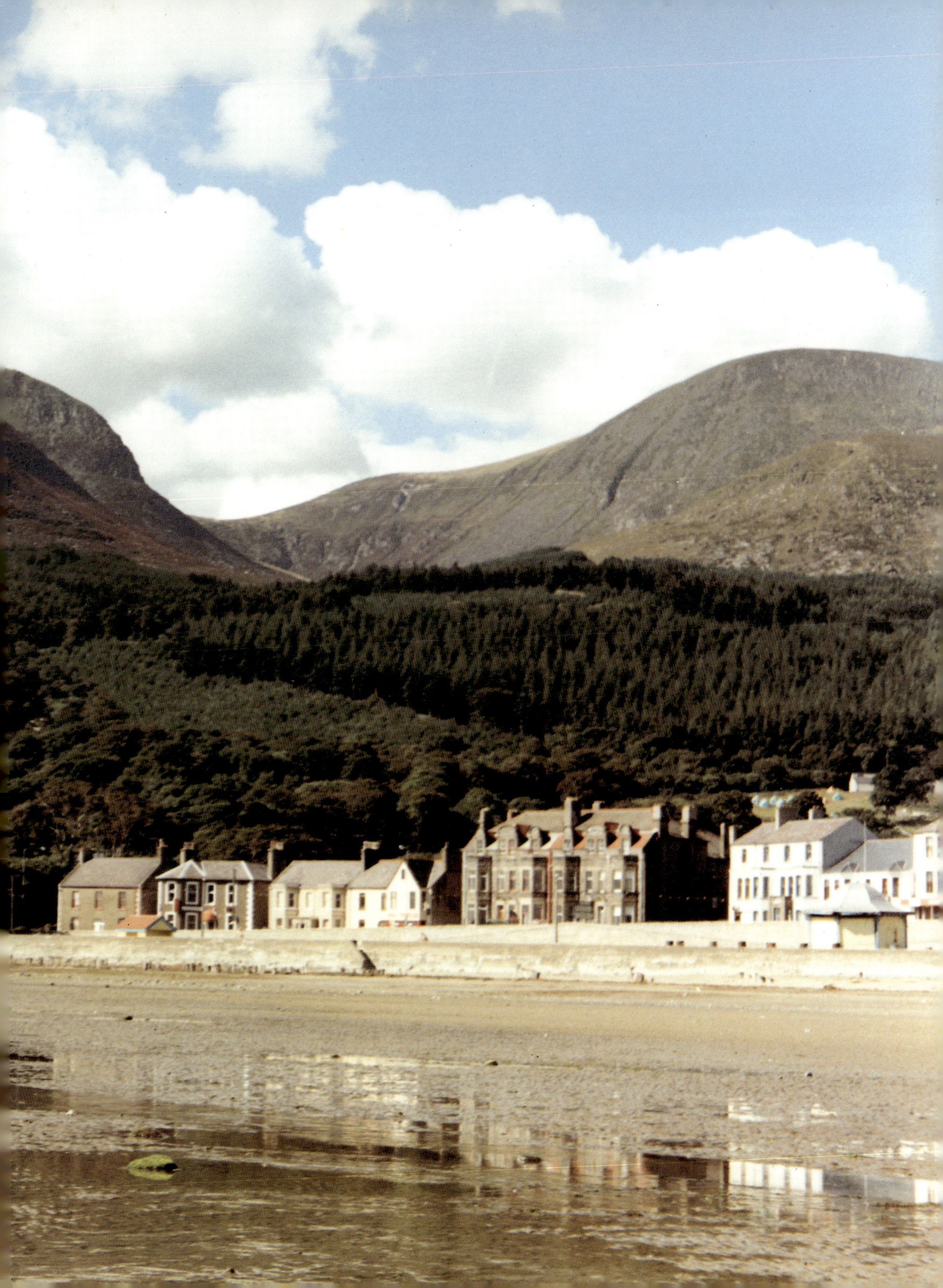

Edwardian Ladies

The first ladies quadrangular international match was held at Newcastle in May 1907 in the two days preceding the L.G.U. Championships. For some years Ireland and England had been the strong sides, with Scotland trailing a little weakly, and this was the first time Wales had fielded a team. Ireland was clearly in fine form on their home ground and won the first golfing Triple Crown, soundly defeating the other three countries. Of the Irish team of seven players, three were from the famous Hezlet family of Portrush, Violet, May and Florence, and Miss Magill from Newcastle.

Following these matches "The Belfast Newsletter" produced some vintage stuff:

"The Irish ladies were not a little elated at their fine series of victories over the sister countries and they are not without strong hopes that one of their countrywomen will gain the coveted title of open champion. The weather was charming. There are few links in the United Kingdom from which can be seen so many beautiful vistas of scenery or views so diversified and picturesque. The rugged and serrated range of mountains lying behind and sheltering the pretty little town loom up in strong contrast to the long stretch of fertile and undulating country beneath, and tower majestically over the broad expanse of sea lying to the eastward. Yesterday the summit of Slieve Donard and the slopes of the lower hills were enshrouded in a shimmering haze through which a strong sun shone somewhat mistily but away to seaward the sky was of

"As a compliment to the United States representatives, the Misses Curtis, the Stars and Stripes was hoisted at the ladies' club house."

a Sicilian blue, flecked with fleecy clouds, and the waves sparkled and danced merrily in the gentle breeze which blew towards the land. The clubhouse has been surrendered to the ladies for the week and mere man is therefore a negligible quantity for the time being. The Slieve Donard Hotel is being well patronised and arrivals from the other side of the channel and from America are charmed with their experiences. As a compliment to the United States representatives, the Misses Curtis, the Stars and Stripes was hoisted at the ladies' clubhouse."

The American visitors would certainly have been gratified had they realised that the famous cup they presented in later years for perpetual challenge between the United States and British Isles would be played for on the same links 61 years later.

May Hezlet. *Isette Pearson (captain of the English team).*

The championship itself was fascinating and culminated in an intriguing final between May and Florence Hezlet, the former winning by 2 and 1. The gentlemen were delighted at such a successful week's golf and, perhaps succumbing to the effects of such prolonged feminine presence the Council, in a gentle surge of blood to the head, elected May Hezlet and Isette Pearson (Captain of the English team) honorary life members of the Club, the only ladies before or since to have perched upon such a dizzy pinnacle!

Braid and Taylor visited Newcastle in the same month and Ben Sayers had been brought over from Scotland to give a second opinion on the links. He actually attended a Council Meeting and, having conferred with Combe and Dr. Magill, their joint deliberations resulted in some further alterations to the links, particularly in the repositioning of bunkers. He was highly critical of the seventh hole, stating that "it is nonsense having a good bunker and then placing the tee so close to it that a child could drive over it". He rearranged it so that it became a one shot hole, the green "to be reached with the brassey or the cleek".

All this was the culmination of much work. Combe appeared satisfied, and announced to Council that the course was ready to be "opened", suggesting that Lord Shaftesbury should do so on May 2.

On April 15, 1908, Council noted:–

"The Home Office had written that they had received His Most Gracious Majesty's permission to extend to us his patronage with the title of Royal".

As he had been in practically every facet of the Club's life, it appears that Combe had been a partial instigator of this one as well, first discussing the possibility with Lord Annesley who in turn approached the Earl of Shaftesbury, well connected in "the proper quarters" in London. Two weeks after the Royal Patronage had been conferred upon the Club, Lord Shaftesbury became Captain, an event perhaps not unconnected with his efforts. In his address to the membership on that occasion he stated that he was greatly honoured but feared that his duties might prevent him from playing golf as often as he would wish. This was the under-statement of 1908, for apart from the following Saturday when he officially opened the long course, "getting a magnificent tee shot in perfect line and distance" he did not attend a Council Meeting until March 1909, when he proposed the young Earl Annesley, later to become President, as his successor.

The No. 2 course

Little had so far been recorded about the additional holes being played on by the ladies. A few certainly existed but considerable work must have been going on in an area near the Club House and on ground earlier released by the re-design of the "Long Course", for immediately after Lord Shaftesbury's opening tee shot, he accompanied Miss Coates,

Miss Curtis of the U.S.A. in action against Violet Hezlet.

Captain of the Ladies Club, to the Ladies Course where nine holes had miraculously appeared and where she performed a similar ceremony "amid much enthusiasm."

```
                                        WHITEHALL,
    159,330/8.
                                        15th April, 1908.

        My Lord,
                I have the honour, by direction of the Secretary of
        State, to inform Your Lordship that the application of the
        Committee of the County Down Golf Club to be allowed to use
        the prefix "Royal" in the name of the Club has been submitted
        to The King, and that His Majesty has been graciously pleased
        to accede to the Committee's request, and to command that
        the Club be known in future by the title "Royal County
        Down Golf Club".
                        I have the honour to be,
                                My Lord,
                                Your Lordship's obedient Servant,

    The Right Honourable
        The Earl of Annesley,
            Castlewellan,
                County Down.
```

Letter granting Royal Patronage.

A delightful contemporary description of their course is worth recording, and it would seem that these holes are virtually the existing "flat nine" on No. 2 Course:—

The lady members of the County Down Club have every reason to congratulate themselves upon the rearrangement of their course. The plan adopted is an admirable one and, shortly described, will result in the delimitation of a portion of the links admirably suited to the fair sex. In the form of an irregular parallelogram, one side of which skirts the railway, the course will be uninterruptedly their own, and embraces within its area sporting possibilities naturally more obvious to the player than to the mere observer. The projected extensions are undoubtedly a very great improvement. What was known as the "Railway" green will be taken in and, after the more important alterations have been made on the links proper, a few days will suffice to complete the changes in contemplation for the benefit of the lady members. There will be no crossing with the larger course and where the two approach each other on the journey homewards, the route lies on parallel lines.

Going to the first hole, the tee is practically behind the last green and the line of play runs down the railway, one good shot being required to reach the green. The second is a nice two shot

"Lord Shaftesbury ... getting a magnificent tee shot in perfect line and distance".

hole to the present "Railway" while the third affords a pretty chip across a couple of banks, the player still following the railway line. The fourth is again a capital two-shot hole, either on to Ward's old green, or near to the gentlemen's "Sheepfold". This stretch has yet to be more fully surveyed but there seems to be little to pick or choose between either alternative, and the decision ultimately come to is certain to be advantageous in every sense of the word. Playing to the fifth, a move is made towards "Old Dundrum" and the sixth is a drive and pitch across the big bunkers to the top of the "Railway" green where there will be two holes. A pretty one-shot hole is the seventh, the green being placed between the three high bunkers guarding the present seventeenth green on the long course. One of these bunkers will, of course, be removed in order that the hole may be visible from the tee but a pot bunker will be left after the bank has been taken down.

The eighth is another fine two shot hole to one of the cross banks on the present eighteenth hole and the ninth is a one-shot drive home to the ladies' clubhouse, landing practically in their back garden. It will thus be seen that while there is nothing phenomenally difficult about these nine holes, there is abundance of variety and, when finished, the ladies may felicitate themselves upon possessing for their own unrestricted enjoyment a truly interesting course.

Not many days after the opening of their course, the ladies arranged a mixed foursome in aid of the Belfast Home for Dogs and Cats. It is not recorded if the event was a success.

Combe's dream   In recognition of his great service to the Club, George Combe was elected an honorary life member in May 1909 and promptly celebrated this by proposing to Council that he should approach the Annesley Estate to acquire more ground. The then Lord Annesley, although Captain of the Club, donned his other hat during negotiations and made it quite clear that such requests would not be granted automatically. He asked, and Council complied, that the hedge outside the Club House be removed at any time if he requested it, and even the gift of some splendid wedding presents did not produce a guarantee of a much needed water supply. Nevertheless by the autumn his Lordship, who in fact had a great affection for the Club, agreed to a new 21 year lease, with additional land at the Dundrum end of the course, for £70 per annum. Nevertheless, it was to be a further 20 years before the forcefulness of Stanley Ferguson brought Combe's dream to realisation.

"Sea pink"

In the summer of that year the greens were badly affected by "sea pink". Council deliberated on letters received from Mr. Dickson (of the well known Ulster family of horticulturalists) recommending weedkiller and from Mr. Carter recommending weeding. They took decisive action, instructing the greenkeeper to weed one green and treat another with weedkiller.

They also resolved at this time that two of their retiring members be ineligible for re-election, thus preventing oligarchic perpetuation.

For some years before the world war of 1914-1918 there had been unease in Irish Golf because of the political situation in the country, and the Club had not entered for many competitions, but the Edwardian taste for a grand dinner was unaffected. The "Belfast Newsletter" devoted three columns to a splendid description of the annual dinner of 1911. After the Loyal Toast, Lord Shaftesbury proposed "Queen Alexandra, the Prince and Princess of Wales, and other members of the Royal Family" which was enriched with the singing of "God Bless the Prince of Wales". In genial vein they then toasted the Golfing Union of Ireland, the Royal County Down Golf Club, and the visitors, to all of which the most eloquent proposals and replies were made. Hair,

On New Year's Eve, 1910, the County Down Stag Hounds met at the steps of the Club House and were entertained by the Captain and Members of Council.

ultimately, was let down, for songs were given by the Earl of Shaftesbury, Colonel Wallace and Mr. R. Woods.

> *"adding considerably to the pleasure of the guests, and the pianoforte accompaniments were artistically provided by Mr. H. F. Ellingford, Mus.Bac., FRCO, who at great inconvenience had made special arrangements to be present for the purpose."*

During the Autumn Meeting of 1911 the Club brought Harry Vardon over to play with some of the members and give exhibition matches. He received £15 for travelling and hotel expenses, plus £8 per day when playing with ordinary members, and £10 per day for exhibition matches. The total cost of the visit was £80.13s.0d, less £25 received from Malone and Bangor Clubs "for the use of Vardon for 2 days".

Council had decided to allow low-handicap members of other clubs to compete in this medal and John Ball had come over from Hoylake. In the medal he achieved an 82 off plus 6 in half a gale. Of the four rounds played by Vardon he recorded 72, two 75s and a 78, the last score in a 40 mile an hour wind. It had been thought that Vardon was not getting great length from the tees but George Combe noted in admiration that he varied between forty and sixty yards further than any of the others, amateur or professional, either with or against the wind, and at the second hole his drive downwind exceeded three hundred yards.

Combe's insatiable desire to improve the course raised its head again and it was clear that he had a deeper purpose in mind when he organised Vardon's visit because suggestions to Council for further course improvements were accepted. Guarantors to the Vardon Fund were called upon to pay ten shillings each. Council was mindful that Combe had spent considerable sums out of his own pocket on his relentless pursuit of improvements to the links and felt this should not be overlooked.

Harry Vardon

The same year brought to the Council a forceful figure, Fred Rogers.

Clubhouse and Garden 1911.

The 7th green, 1911. Now a heathery area on the left of the 1st green.

The 8th hole, 1911. The green lay at the base of what is now the 9th hill.

The 13th green, 1911.

The 16th hole, 1911.

He combined executive ability with valuable service as Captain and Honorary Secretary. At the time he joined the Council the Club was in the midst of its most formative years and in addition to some of the old hands who were still active such as Dr. Magill, George Combe, Fred Hoey and F. L. Heyn, it now included younger men such as Sir George Clark and Harold Coates. All were great contributors and some were scratch golfers. It is somewhat surprising, therefore, to read in a minute that "G. Clark complained of the difficulty of playing on the ladies' course." The difficulty was probably the condition of the fairways, not the lay-out, for Sir George was a good player. The green committee must have been stung into action for the next Council minute recorded laconically, "G. Combe reported alterations to the ladies' course."

Fred Rogers – "that affable Honorary Secretary".

Harold Hilton

The Irish Open Championship of 1912 produced an interesting field and some fine golf. A special golfing correspondent reviewed the prospects for the Tournament thus:—

The Clark Cup

"Mr. Hilton has suffered a somewhat unexpected defeat in the American golf championship and Irish golfers will wait with interest his own story of how, on a thirtysix holes match, he should so far relapse as to be at one time seven holes down to an absolutely unknown player. Meantime, we are now deeply interested in Irish affairs and our championship, which opens on Monday at Newcastle, promises to be the finest amateur event we have ever had in the Island. The entry is less in numbers than a year ago but in point of class there has never been anything so good. To divide the draw into four sections, we have in the top division Mr. F. S. Bond, who so nearly defeated Mr. Ball at Westward Ho!, and Mr. Charles B. Macfarlane, who has proved himself one of the most brilliant amateurs of the year. In the second section we have Mr. John Ball, Mr. Craig, the Irish close champion, and the Honourable Michael Scott.

In the third section we have Mr. Gordon Lockhart, Mr. Frank Carr, Mr. Cairnes, Mr. D. Forster, and Mr. H. E. Reade. In the last section we have Mr. Munn and Mr. C. Palmer. I

have picked out these names to show how well the big men have been distributed and what a magnificent prospect there is for a semi-final. Mr. Munn has been remarkably well drawn and ought to get to the semi-final stage. If Gordon Lockhart is in form at all he should beat Frank Carr, and the lengthy Scotsman is quite good enough for any other player in this section. Mr. Ball has been in the Island for over a week on holiday and one never knows what mood he may be in. The Honourable Michael Scott is one of the big chances of the meeting. Since last September Mr. Scott has improved very greatly. In the top section little Macfarlane, a perfect master of his clubs and one of the most delightful players to watch, should easily get through to the penultimate stage. Altogether the championship has the very best of prospects.

Lionel Munn driving from the 7th tee. Irish Open, 1912.

Many of the seeds, such as John Ball and A. H. Craig, tumbled early on and the surprise of the championship came when Lionel Munn was beaten by Gordon Lockhart — subsequently professional at Gleneagles — of Prestwick St. Nicholas, a match characterised by sensational putting, both players having played 30 shots for the last nine holes. In the 36 hole final Lockhart beat P. G. Jenkins of Troon, conveniently near the club house, by eleven and nine.

Towards the end of 1912 the Council put on record their opinion, and conveyed it to the annual meeting of the Golfing Union of Ireland, that the Irish Amateur Championship should be abolished. Under the circumstances it had not been a surprising view to hold for the entries that year at Castlerock had dropped to 31. However, this may have been something to do with a venue so far North for in 1913 at Portmarnock they had increased to 67 when Lionel Munn achieved the third of his four victories. His fourth was at Hermitage the next year when he beat Lord Annesley in the final.

In the Spring of 1913 George Combe fell ill and was absent from the Club for some time. Council were doubtful about his return and took the

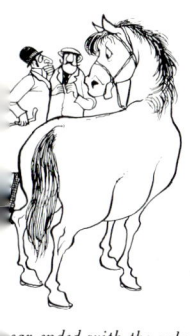

John Ball in trouble at the 6th. The Irish Open, 1912.

opportunity to curb his sometimes dictatorial ways by appointing Lord Annesley as convenor of the Green Committee. Combe was deeply hurt and did not appear in the Club for many years afterwards. This was an unfortunate conclusion to so many years of devoted interest, and although he was autocratic no one could derogate his great achievements. The Club and Irish Golf are much in his debt.

Membership was by now widely spread, with many resident in both England and Scotland and quite a number overseas. July of that year saw new overseas members elected, an event irreverently depicted in the suggestion book by an uneasy Huw Wallace.

Electric light had been installed in 1911 after a great deal of protracted argument and the final condemnation of an unsatisfactory and very dubious system of oil lighting. Before the lights began to go out all over Europe Council agreed to extend light to the Ladies Club and the professional was to be "lit up" for £2.10s.0d a year to which was to be added "a heating radiator and an outside lamp."

That year the Annual Dinner was held in a tastefully re-decorated Clubhouse, and members and visitors were pleasantly impressed by "the electric lighting."

Sir James Henderson, one of the original members, died in the Spring of 1914, as did The Rt Hon. Thomas Sinclair, the Father of Irish Golf. And so, with George Combe having departed, the Old Guard, who had given so much in the first 25 years of the Club's life, was beginning to disappear.

"... an event irreverently depicted by an uneasy Huw Wallace".

War — and the Club Poet

When the war which did not end all wars began in 1914 many members went to the colours and it became an exceedingly difficult time for all golf clubs. Apart from its contribution in terms of membership of the forces the Club took part in all the war enterprises open to it, including the Prince of Wales Relief Fund, the Ulster Volunteer Force Hospitals, and joint financing of the local Soldiers' Home in Newcastle.

In the early part of December 1914 it received a great blow when its President, Lord Annesley, was lost when the 'plane in which he was travelling to France disappeared over the Channel. Although he had lost an eye in an accident while at Cambridge, he had become one of the most talented golfers in Ireland, and in the few years leading up to the war a real driving force in the Club, chairing the Green Committee with vigour and imagination from George Combe's retirement until he left for the war. Between 1913 and the early part of 1914 he had continued Combe's inexhaustible search for improvements and at the Annual General Meeting of 1914 it was reported that he had succeeded in making the course less "blind" at six holes, enlarged ten tees and made 9 new ones, an immense piece of "winter work". He personally supervised all of it, often being present on the course before seven in the morning, and working long hours with his men — until his departure to the war — on the construction of what became known as Lord Annesley's Path. It is virtually unchanged today and runs over the marshy ground in front of the fifteenth tee.

Francis, 6th Earl Annesley, 2nd President of the Club.

The Earl Annesley Cup

Early in 1915 the Club joined with the Ladies Club and gave a concert in the Rosemary Hall, Belfast, for 120 wounded soldiers from all

the hospitals in Belfast and surrounding area who were "conveyed to the vicinity of the hall in special tramcars kindly supplied by the City Corporation". Fred Rogers welcomed his guests with a rousing speech and at an interval for tea part way through the concert each soldier was "made the recipient of three very useful gifts — a box of handkerchiefs, an instantaneous lighter and a small unbreakable mirror, the presentations being gracefully made by Miss Ewing". It is difficult not to smile gently at a contemporary description of the second half of this Edwardian occasion:—

> "The remainder of the entertainment programme was then given. The musical and other numbers were very kindly arranged by Mr. W. M. McMullan and were quite a strong feature of the proceedings, every item being most enthusiastically encored. Pianoforte solos by the gifted artiste Mr. J. H. MacBratney were most tastefully rendered and his accompaniments were very pleasing throughout. There were songs by Corporal Wrigley, 9th Devons; Private Lambert, 20th Canadians; Mr. R. M. Patterson, Mr. W. M. McMullan and Mr. W. Dick; violin solos by Lance-Corporal Watson, King's Liverpool Regiment, and Mr. W. B. Haughton; recitations by Miss C. McIldowie and Mr. G. B. Hanna; and a dance by Private Heaney, Royal Irish Rifles."

During the war years there was naturally a big fall in income from visitors and no competitions were held. In 1915 the Steward was authorised to charge 2 shillings for lunch owing to increases in the price of all food, and the green keeper, George Reid, was granted £2 "for his attention to the greens from attacks by the suffragettes."

"... *for his attention to the greens from attacks of the suffragettes.*"

One of the few excitements of the war years was the wreck of the Dutch vessel *"Fulvia"* whose survivors were cared for in the Club House by the Steward, Howden, and his wife.

The military authorities were granted permission to dig trenches on waste ground on the course so that the soldiers stationed temporarily in Newcastle could train. These are still to be found between the fourth tee on number 1 course and ninth hole on number 2 course. Set in such idyllic surroundings they must have presented a prospect of war very different to the ghastly scenes the young soldiers were soon to meet in the battlefields of Flanders.

May 1915 saw Wilson Smyth taking his seat on Council for the first time. He was to become a driving force in Irish Golf and a tower of strength and determination in the Club. Many years later it was said of him that he ruled the Club with a rod of iron for the "last 25 years of his life and for ten years after his death". More will be said of him later but his contribution and that of his daughter and sons were signal in the life and development of both Clubs.

During the war, subtleties of rank were shown when it was ruled that election without entrance fee applied only to Curates and that "Rectors, Parish Priests and other higher ranks of the clergy come in as ordinary members". Also

> "that any gentleman defaulting in his subscription whose name has been removed from the list of members will not be permitted to play on the links as a visitor."

Lady Mabel Annesley's Agent sought part of the ladies' course for the Urban District Council to use as an allotment. This apparent contribution to the war effort was actually the signal for more than a decade of delicate, and indeed sometimes bitter, negotiations, culminating in the final purchase of the land. The Club replied frostily that "the ground was most unsuitable, as the best of it has only three inches of soil, most of it touching sand. Additionally, it would destroy 3 of the ladies' greens, thus practically ruining their course". The Estate did not pursue this further, presumably sensing that vegetables grown in three inches of soil could only be of dubious quality.

The Roll of Honour in the hall includes those who fell at the Somme in 1916 when the flower of young Ulster was hacked at the stem. At one period during the war almost a third of the membership was serving and the Victory Dinner of 1919 must have been one of mixed emotions.

Nevertheless, despite austere times, the Club had a credit balance when peace was restored and a long waiting list for membership. Council agreed to resume competitions and accepted the Ladies Championship in 1920. It had been an anxious time, and the Ladies Golf Union were timid about coming to Ireland owing to disturbed conditions in some parts of the island but, as a result of representations by Hugh Kelly, who was at that time a Vice-President of the L.G.U., and by Fred Hoey, they went on with their plans and the championship proved a great success, Miss Cecil Leitch beating Miss Griffiths in the final.

The Victory Cup

The Club was in good heart again and at the end of 1920 membership was recorded as 332 ordinary, 70 outport and 86 others. Social life was also back to normal and one of the biggest accounts for the year appears to have been with the Old Bushmills Distillery Company.

"Pipe cleaners"

At the annual meeting of 1921 Wilson Smyth was elected captain for the first time and a few months later won the Irish Open Amateur Championship on his home course, beating Joseph Gorry of Naas by 2 holes. It had been a championship of turn-ups in the earlier rounds with E. F. Carter, Charles Hezlet and Guy Ellis all succumbing when perhaps they ought not to have done, and Alfie Lowe of Malone beating

Joseph Gorry.

Wilson Smyth.

his own club champion by 8 and 7. But none of this detracts in any way from Smyth's victory. He had been five down at the 8th in the final and was in considerable pain from a strained muscle in his side. Nevertheless, severely strapped after the lunch interval by Hardy Greer, the eminent gynaecologist, he fought back tenaciously and went into the lead at the 16th. At the 17th the referee, the Rev. J. L. Morrow (Honorary Secretary of the Golfing Union of Ireland) picked up a seagull's feather and Gorry claimed the hole, maintaining that it had been within a club's length of Smyth's ball. "Excellent pipe cleaners, these feathers", remarked the reverend gentleman, and disallowed the claim. The local press quoted that the crowd, understandably perhaps just a shade partisan, "gave Smyth a tremendous ovation, and Gorry a cordial cheer".

In September the Club held a dinner in his honour at which he was presented with a gold-mounted hunting crop. This was a pleasant gesture from the members, acknowledging his wider sporting activities, for he was also a keen huntsman and Master of the Iveagh Harriers.

In the same month the Green Committee reported to Council that their horse was "worn out".

There were regular matches against the Services, and the Army in Ulster presented a fine cup which was first played for in 1922. From time to time they had some difficulty in fielding a full team and called in the other Services. On one occasion they prevailed upon Flying Officer Craik to fly from Baldonnel, still occupied by the R.A.F., with the aim of landing at Aldergrove. However, fog shrouded the airport and in a minor misjudgment his aircraft finished in Lough Neagh. Providentially

.. in a minor misjudgment his aircraft finished in Lough Neagh.

The short 4th, looking south from the medal tee.

The 9th fairway and green.

he was not far from the shore and when he surfaced his cries were heard by the ground staff who were able to retrieve both Craik and clubs. Nothing daunted, he came on to Newcastle to play and holed in one at the 6th with a gale of wind behind him.

In the Irish Ladies Close Championship of 1922 Miss Daisy Ferguson, who was later to make such an enormous contribution to golf in the British Isles, culminating in captaincy of the Curtis Cup Team, but who was then only 17 and appearing in her first championship, had an intriguing incident in her first round match against Mrs. Warner of Hermitage.

"Miss Ferguson was one up at the 16th, and bunkered. There was no sign of the ball, the most prominent object in the hazard being a cardboard hat box, appropriate enough in other circumstances, but not in a golf championship. Under this strange obstacle the ball had coyly hidden itself and could only be seen by the player getting down almost flat on the ground. Miss Ferguson gallantly played box and ball simultaneously, but to no avail, for she lost the hole and the match was squared. The 18th saw the end of an exciting struggle and the County Down lady played it very well indeed, showing no signs of a breakdown for which she might have been excused after losing so commanding a lead as 5 up at the turn."

"... *gallantly played box and ball simultaneously.*"

The minutes of May 1922 record a letter from Denis Sinclair, son of Sir Thomas Sinclair (the Father of Irish golf) advising that he had won the International Trophy at Biarritz and would like to present the replica to Royal County Down. As a replica it is, therefore, the smallest of the Club's trophies, but it was a most generous gesture and his gift is now played for in April each year by the Past Captains, prior to the dinner at which they formally approve the nomination of their successor in office.

"The old 4th green, which lay just short of the existing 5th".

By now "George Combe's course" was nearly complete but it included virtually none of the present championship tees. A contemporary map of the course which was reproduced at the time of

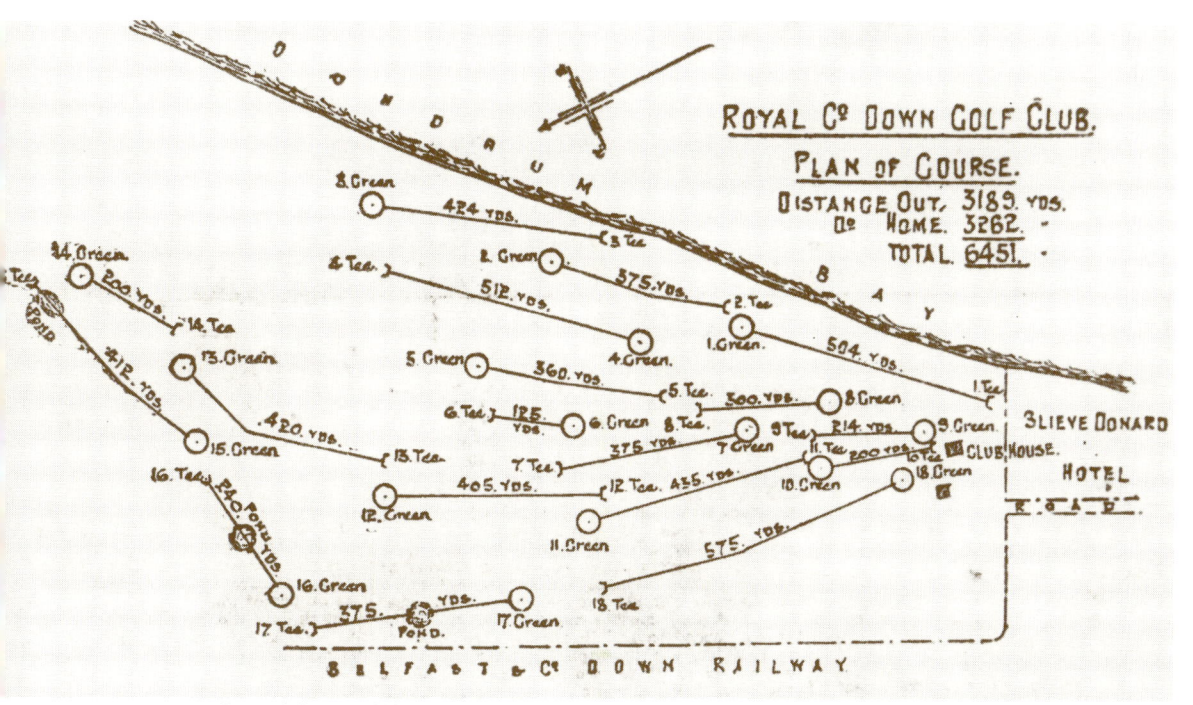

Plan of Course 1923.

the Irish Open Amateur of 1923 shows the second nine not vastly different from today's course in general layout but the first nine were still to see significant changes.

Willie Smyth (son of Wilson) who was later to follow his father as Captain and Honorary Secretary, recalls that the first hole was much as it is now. The second shot to hole number two was completely blind, and since 1921 three attempts were made over the years to correct this failing. Initially the bank in front of the green was lowered in the middle, then the sunken gathering green was raised at the back and levelled, and lastly the hollows of a somewhat undulating fairway were filled in and the whole fairway raised slightly. The third hole did not differ greatly from today but the present fourth did not exist at all. It was then played as a long hole of over 500 yards from a tee on the left of the existing 4th tee (and sometimes visible today as a square of longer and finer grass) to a green short of the present 5th green. The 5th hole (present 6th) was played to a long narrow green which began just over the cross bunker between the bank on the right and a very high mound on the left, somewhat similar to the 7th at Lahinch. The 6th was roughly the present 7th, and the 7th was played from the existing 8th tee to a green over the cross bunkers and down to the left on flat ground near the 1st green. Then followed two holes which would certainly not

The Biarritz Cup.

The old 7th green, lying in low ground west of the existing 1st.

The old 8th green, at the bottom of the present 9th hill.

have been rated as highly today but which were a tremendous challenge in the early golfing days. The 8th was a completely blind one shot hole played from the existing lower 9th tee to a green which can still be seen today just over and at the base of the hill. The 9th was again a blind one-shotter, played from a tee in the middle of the existing 9th fairway, over the hill, (no whins existed on the course then) and on to the present putting green. A contemporary description of the course declared that "considerable skill in putting was necessary to obtain a par 3". Despite many requests over the years to level it Council has remained firm that the members should still be able to putt on one of the very early and largely unaltered greens.

This, then, was the course on which the Irish Open Amateur was played once more in 1923 when, as the "Belfast News Letter" put it:

> "Captain G. N. C. Martin (Royal Portrush) is for the second time the winner of this championship, having defeated his club-mate, Major C. O. Hezlet, by one up over 36 holes in the best final that has ever been seen in Irish Golf".

" ... the first green, where Martin holed a long put for a 3".

James Henderson, in his earlier history of the Club, said it was the most perfect display of golf he had ever seen in an amateur championship. It was, indeed, a memorable occasion and one cannot do better than quote the "News Letter's" vivid description of the morning round:—

"The first round provided the best exhibition of golf ever seen in a championship in Ireland. It was "phenomenal stuff" as one ardent, and perspiring, spectator phrased it, and he was not exaggerating. Captain Martin was round in approximately 70 and his opponent in 74, and the best ball was 65. Figures, however, convey but little idea of the quality of the play. The thrills started at the first hole where Martin holed a long putt for a 3.

Hezlet and Martin leaving the first tee.

The hole measures 504 yards. To such a state has the modern golf ball reduced our golf courses. Then Hezlet got a three at the second, and Martin secured another 3 at the third hole, which measures 424 yards. This was a terrific beginning and people asked themselves when was it going to end. There were, however, more fireworks to come.

After more or less conventional play from the 4th to the 7th, inclusive, during which Martin was lucky to win the pitch hole, there came yet another 3, this time at the 8th, and this put Martin 2 up. Up to this point Hezlet had been outdriving his opponent, as, indeed was expected but his second shots were not quite so accurate as they had been during the week. At the 9th Hezlet was stymied again — the first occasion being at the 6th — but he deftly lofted his ball into the hole with a mashie niblick, and so stood only one down. This clever stroke was the most courageous of the day.

The "crazy stuff" was once more in evidence when they turned for home, for Martin holed a chip shot from the far edge of the tenth green for a 2 to win the hole, which most of the spectators thought he would lose, and followed this up by a gorgeous 3 at the 11th. Hezlet played both holes quite well, getting a 3 and a 4. A half in 4 at the 12th followed and then it became Hezlet's turn to beat par, for he holed the 13th (the "round the corner" hole) in 3, reducing his opponent's lead to 2 up. Halves followed at the 14th and 15th, Hezlet missing a good chance of winning the 15th, but being weak with his putting. The last two holes of the round were rather poorly played, in comparison with what had gone before. Martin won the 17th and Hezlet the 18th, and so the round finished with Martin 2 up.

During the whole course of the round Major Hezlet was "up against it", but he played with great courage, and the fact that he was only 2 down to such great golf speaks volumes for the quality of his own play.

Captain Martin played with superlative confidence and ease. He hit only about three from fair to bad shots during the round and his short game was a treat to witness. He holed three long putts and one approach, which might be called lucky or skilful according to taste, but it may be said quite impartially that the ball, on these occasions, never looked like going anywhere else than into the bottom of the hole.

One other interesting feature of the round may be noted. It took only two hours and sixteen minutes to accomplish. Neither of the two players wasted any time over the shots. There was no elaborate studying of the line and none of those painful pauses which have been experienced in other finals when the competitors were examining the atmospheric conditions, or in other ways delaying the proceedings in the belief that such meticulous care was necessary for the successful accomplishment of their strokes. Captain Martin and Major Hezlet yesterday demonstrated not only how to play good golf but showed how unnecessary it is for golfers in practice to toil over their game as if their lives depended on each stroke."

The Coronation Cup

"a toy"

Fred Hoey, who had retired as Honorary Secretary the previous year, and no longer a young man, followed the entire match, perspiring freely, at what must have seemed to him a half gallop and muttering tersely, "Making a toy of the course".

After the war the financial affairs of the Club, although sound, were a little haphazard, and Council asked W. B. Haughton to act as Honorary Treasurer. This he willingly did, presenting the affairs of the club regularly and lucidly to Council, clearly to their great relief. Willie Haughton was a much loved character and became known as The Club Poet. His contribution was a significant one, not only with financial guidance, but his opinions were respected and acted upon on course and

W. B. Haughton.

club house improvements. His literary gems appeared when he wished to mark a special occasion, but more often as a gentle jibe at a Committee decision. His poems were beautifully and cleverly illustrated by Huw Wallace, son of Colonel R. H. Wallace, who had contributed so much to the early life of the club.

He served on Council for over fifteen years, and on his death an obituary was added to the book which contains his poems and is worth recording to show the great affection in which he was held.

"Were it possible to recall all the wits and beauties of whom no human memory now remains, the gifts and graces of men and women now forgotten, were it possible by some magic formula to recall all these — all the handsome and clever faces, the genial humorists, the whimsical talkers, the gay, the satirical, the facetious tongues — were all these restored to us, what a delightful company would be assembled! What a society would be ours! Alas! the talents and the charms that are gone, and nothing now left to show for them!

Against this wastage of time, though, little can be done. Yet what little is worth doing. This book cannot indeed restore Willie Haughton to his friends — the brown, penetrating eyes, the strong, frank, kindly, humorous countenance, the breadth and sanity of mind, the sense of fun, the keen appreciation of the follies and foibles of man, and the absurdities of things. A man may have accomplishments and be little beloved; he may paint or play divinely on stringed instruments, or we may admire his skills and yet take no pleasure in his society. But when his personal qualities, his turn of speech, his smile, or even his eccentricities delight us, we take him to our hearts.

So it is with Willie Haughton, the best known figure, I fancy, for many years among our Members."

Interim measure

But back to the course again.

Rumblings had been developing, and were acknowledged fair, that the ladies' course should be enlarged to 18 holes. Dr. Magill had the radical suggestion of abandoning the 14th and 17th holes on the Long Course and replace them on ground to the east of the existing 13th. By doing this, he argued, the Ladies Course could easily be extended to 18 holes and within the same area. The Green Committee were opposed to giving up so much land on the Long Course and Council agreed to an interim measure by constructing five or six new holes on the west of the existing 12th and 13th.

In 1924 the Green Committee was chaired by W. H. K. (Skipper) Lowry, who had been a Captain in the Merchant Navy, trading in the Far East in Joseph Conrad country. He had retired to Newcastle and lived in Wilmar, now a restaurant, which he filled with Eastern china and furniture. He was not a good golfer, but the kindest of men, and it was sometimes hard to curb his great enthusiasm when he felt a certain course of action was needed for the greater benefit of the links. Such an occasion arose in the Spring of 1924 when he took to heart the much earlier opinion of Old Tom Morris that the only way to treat a links course was with "Sand, sand, an' mair sand". This compelled Willie Haughton and Huw Wallace to commit their first epic to the book which, up to that point, had been the suggestion book.

Lines written on Sand
Inscribed with the utmost disrespect to the GREEN Committee.

1

In the spring I often wonder
As I saunter Cleek in hand
Why the Green Committee's fancies
Lightly turn to thoughts of sand.

—2—

In the spring a soft virescence
Tints the fairways bright & gay
Lo! next Saturday we find we're
In the bally consommé!

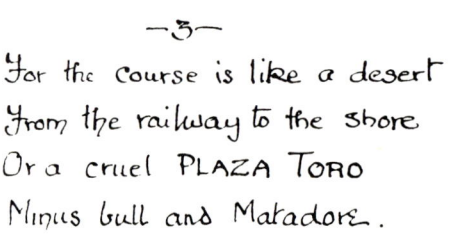

—3—

For the course is like a desert
From the railway to the shore
Or a cruel PLAZA TORO
Minus bull and Matadore.

— 4 —

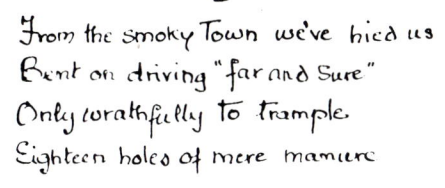

From the smoky Town we've hied us
Bent on driving "far and sure"
Only wrathfully to trample
Eighteen holes of mere manure

"Coals to Newcastle".

— 5 —

In a landscape unfamiliar
Caverns yawn on every hand
Mutely crying "Brutal Skipper
Give us back our tons of SAND!"

— 6 —

On this page (supplied to those who
Think they've something to suggest)
I exhort the Green Committee.
"Give the blooming course a rest"

"BLOOD and SAND"

—7—
Oh All Highest Green Convenor!
Thou of stern majestic mien
I implore you for a season
Discontinue to convene!

Excavations at the 13th Hole.

Prepared for all emergencies.

—8—
With the "Carpenter and Walrus"
In the Spring I take my stand
For " like anything I weep to
See such quantities of SAND".

Darwinism. or:—
An example of the doctrine of Environment.

The Green Convenor appended his own Biblical warning:—

Read Provʳ 27ᵗʰ v3ʳᵈ

{ "A stone is heavy, and sand weighty, but a Fool's wrath is heavier than them both"

Wᵐ Lowry
Convener of Green Committee

which spurred Haughton and Wallace to further inspiration the following week:—

Re "Proverbs XXVII. 3." (see preceeding page)

O jesters and suggesters pause to think
What may ensue when rashly you have dip't your
Presumptuous goose-quills in the clubhouse ink —
You'll find yourselves "K.O." by Holy Scripture!

See what befel us ("Hu" and me) last week
A kick we made re "SAND" with small compunction
And get for thanks a wallop on the beak
From Solomon and "Skipper" in conjunction.—

Had I been Solomon I would have writ
In terminology sententious, flow'ry
"The weight of Sand et cet'ra's great — but it
"Is gossamer compared with Wm. Lowry"!

W. B. H.
Mch 18. x

This controversy must please cease, our columns are not intended for religious controversy, or for idle and unseemly persiflage —

EDITOR, "Suggestion Book.

Straightness, Charm and the Lease

As a championship course Newcastle had, almost from its inception, been regarded as one of the greats but was justly criticised on two counts. Firstly, because of the number of "gathering" greens, and secondly, and more severely, for the number of blind and semi-blind shots to the greens. Wilson Smyth was very conscious of this and it was he who had the vision and energy to continue George Combe's great search for perfection. In 1926 he and C. S. Harden, who was at that time Secretary of the Malone Club in Belfast, and who had been appointed Curator of the links at Newcastle to help and advise on course maintenance, brought H. S. Colt over from England to try and devise a means between them of eliminating these weaknesses. Colt brought with him Willie Murray, one of the earliest Walker Cup players.

"Beside the 18th green was a mound as high as the 10th tee".

The scheme they jointly presented to Council was approved and implemented during the next few years. This consisted of a new fourth hole, roughly as it is now, new cross bunkers and green for the eight hole (then the 7th) and a new ninth hole played as a blind tee shot from today's top tee to the present green set behind new cross bunkers. Only when these were fully playable were the old 7th, 8th and 9th greens abandoned. He and Harden also changed the 11th and 18th greens to those we play on today. The 11th green had been in a gathering hollow beyond and to the left of the existing green and the 18th green was just about where the professional's shop is today. Beside this green was a mound as high as the 10th tee and on which the caddies perched, refusing to move, while on strike during an earlier Ladies Championship. A shot to the 18th green which was on the strong side dropped over the edge of the green and was out of bounds on the road.

Blind spot   The changes to eliminate the gathering greens and reduce the blind shots met with universal approval in the golfing world. Nevertheless, Wilson Smyth was still not happy, particularly with the 8th green, which was on a steep slope just behind the cross bunkers. It was extremely difficult to hold a second shot on the putting surface and an attempt to alter its contours by lessening the slope failed to produce any significant improvement. Smyth led his head greenkeeper, John McCavery, and staff, throughout the winter months levelling rough ground some forty yards behind the green and was then able to put the putting surface which exists today into commission.

The old 6th green.

During some of the following winters three more changes were made which resulted in the course as it is played today. The 12th hole was lengthened by taking the green back some 50 yards, the 15th hole was lengthened (after the 1939-45 war) by 60 yards in the same way, and the most difficult of his final improvements was the construction of the present sixth green and its surrounds. It was a major operation because a large hill existed to the left of the old green, and he was always proud that he had fashioned the new green and its surrounds from what he termed "a pile of old sand".

Later in 1924, and whether or not as a result of the sand committed to the course by Skipper Lowry, there was a problem with weeds, and the minutes record that "the weeding of the course by caddies, as arranged, was being proceeded with". This may not have been entirely successful for a tender for the grazing of sheep on the course was accepted "the maximum number at any one time to be 250 and to be removed from the course on competition days or whenever requested." Eleven years later sheep were put on the course again, but this time for seven months of the year for which the Club received £5 a month "on condition they were removed on Sundays and during competitions".

40 years The same year the House Committee brought forward a scheme for alterations to the Club House but Council rejected it and asked them to prepare alternative plans on a more modest scale. This resulted in a tender of £1,550 being accepted for alterations to the Club House, caddie master's office, professional's shop, and visitors dressing room. In those days these latter buildings were a rather rambling collection of apartments just below and to the west of the tenth tee. It would be 40 years before more ambitious plans for a major Club House alteration were implemented and a further 20 before another extension and major refurbishment were approved and completed in 1988.

The Captain during 1924 was Arthur T. Herdman, an original member of the Club and, although not a good golfer, an immense character socially. Known as "The Scrubber", James Henderson noted that:

> "with his monocle, his perfectly groomed appearance, his air of polite interest, Arthur Herdman might have passed for a dilettante but he had a shrewd and active brain, a gift of choice language and an incisive and at times blistering wit. To hear him speak at a Club dinner in the most polished style, with taste and discrimination, and then in a twinkling change to a robust diatribe in the Ulster dialect was a never-to-be-forgotten experience".

Guy Ellis, Captain in 1926 and 1927, from Horace Hutchinson's 'Book of Golf and Golfers', with "the face pointing straight to Heaven."

Over the years the Club has been fortunate in its Captains, each bringing his own talents to the office and each acknowledging when it was over that the experience had been a unique and heartwarming one. Herdman was followed in office by Stanley Ferguson in 1925 and H. G. B. Ellis in 1926 and 1927.

Ferguson's contribution to the Club was, in its own way, perhaps one of the most significant of any member, and more will be said of it later, but Ellis' was also outstanding. Additionally, he was a golfer of immense talent whose prowess was renowned among all who played. He had been a close friend of Bernard Darwin and they had golfed together as boys at Eton, and later against one another at University. They were both members of the first Oxford and Cambridge Golfing Society tour of America in 1903 when golf there was still in its teens and when the rubber-core ball had barely been in use for twelve months.

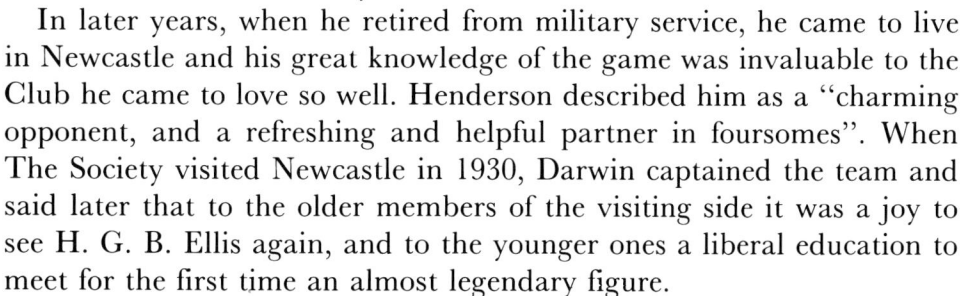

The Granville Cup

In later years, when he retired from military service, he came to live in Newcastle and his great knowledge of the game was invaluable to the Club he came to love so well. Henderson described him as a "charming opponent, and a refreshing and helpful partner in foursomes". When The Society visited Newcastle in 1930, Darwin captained the team and said later that to the older members of the visiting side it was a joy to see H. G. B. Ellis again, and to the younger ones a liberal education to meet for the first time an almost legendary figure.

Bernard Darwin

When Guy Ellis died in 1947, Darwin wrote thus in "Country Life" of his old friend:—

I do not know whether it is merely a senile delusion but it seems to me that today people talk less of famous straight drivers than they used to.

The subject comes into my head because one whom many of my generation believe to have been the straightest of all drivers, Guy Ellis, has lately died and, as he was a very old friend of mine — we used to play together at Eton — and a truly remarkable golfer, I should like to say a little about him. He was one of those who become legends, not merely in their lifetimes, but in their early youth: The legend has now grown rather faint, and many readers may never even have heard of him. When I say he was the straightest of all, I have illustrious authority on my side. I am sure I have told before (perhaps I have now said everything before) how people were one day asking the sage of Walton Heath (James Braid) who was the straightest driver he had ever seen. They suggested various names, at one and all of which he shook his head and then he gave his own quite positive answer: Guy Ellis. There may have been others whose ball finished as often or nearly as often in the middle of the course but there was none, I think, whose ball flew so absolutely straight from point to point. It really did fly, to use a well-worn simile, like a ruled line.

As far as I know the only photographs of him in the act of driving are to be found in The Book of Golf and Golfers by Horace Hutchinson, published in 1899, and there, incidentally, Horace says exactly what Braid said later: "he is without exception the straightest driver that the writer ever saw, and in the opinion of most of those who know his game he is deemed the straightest in the world."

The Army Cup

I have been looking at these pictures yet again to see if there is any clue to be gained. At the top of the swing the face of the club is pointing straight to heaven, most pronouncedly "shut". I cannot recall — perhaps I was unobservant — that it was markedly so in real life and I wonder whether Guy, who had a most impish and irreverant sense of humour, was amusing himself at the photographer's expense. However this may be, the picture is entirely characteristic and I have only to shut my eyes to see it most vividly.

The rest of Guy's game was likewise intensely accurate and, this being so, I cannot say why he did not win all sorts of things, as he certainly ought to have done. He loved the game for its own sake, and loved to play it as well as he could, but I suppose he lacked some workaday "will to victory". It amused him to win his matches by the smallest possible margin. In both our two University matches he won by a single hole from Canbridge players whom, with all possible respect for them, he could have beaten by more. A year or two later somebody gently chaffed him on this peculiarity. That was on the morning of a Woking match against Oxford and in the afternoon he beat his luckless undergraduate opponent by sixteen holes.

The story was told of him — I do not know if there is any truth in it — that he was beating the record of a course by many strokes and that, this fact being rashly pointed out to him, he instantly picked up his ball. Possibly it was invented, but it well might have been true, for no man could predict his antics. Such a temperament did not make for ordinary, commonplace success. It did make of him a delightful, if occasionally embarrassing, companion. He was on of the most amusing of after-dinner speakers and had a brain stored with all manner of curious and interesting information. All who know him were fond of him and retained for him in their minds a particular little niche of his own. His contemporaries, a now dwindling band, will always regard him as one of the essentially great players, and so I have tried to pay this halting little tribute to his memory."

Coastal erosion

The perennial problem of coastal erosion raised its head again in the mid-20s. It was common for sand and shingle to be removed in cartloads and the Club had no power to stop it. Fred Rogers, the forceful Honorary Secretary of the day, visited the Board of Trade in London and persuaded them to send an inspector to Ireland. Following a public enquiry, the Club was able to secure a lease from the Crown of the land lying above mean high water mark and stretching from the southern boundary of the Slieve Donard Hotel to the northern end of the course. Notices prohibiting the further removal of sand were exhibited and work began under Harden's supervision to strengthen the sandhills by planting. Cart loads of rooted grass, known by the locals as "quickeny" grass, was brought from the impoverished land near the village of Maghera and thrived in the sand, but it was many years before there was any real improvememt, and indeed the whims of nature have made it an ongoing and worrying problem. The Club still possesses the Crown Lease of the foreshore although it is a great deal more costly today.

Fred Hoey died in 1927. His had been a guiding hand for more than 30 years. Honorary Secretary for more than eighteen years, and Captain three times, he had made a powerful contribution, but he had taught his successor well and Fred Rogers, who had taken office as Honorary

Secretary in 1923, was to remain so until 1934. In his own way, he was just as forceful and, although he was held in great esteem by the membership, he stood no nonsense. On one occasion in the late twenties he "banished" two members to the number 2 course for a month until they "learned to play at a greater speed". Apparently they did so without argument.

The Silver Casket and Scrolls of the Annesley Cup.

Gallic charm

In May of the same year the British Ladies Championship came back to Royal County Down after an absence of seven years. On the previous occasion Miss Cecil Leitch had won but this time neither she nor Joyce Wethered were present, both of whom were the most powerful and consistent players of the day. Nevertheless this in no way detracts from the performance of the winner, Mlle. Simone Thion de la Chaume of the St. Cloud Club, Paris, who defeated Miss Dorothy Pearson (Nevill, Turnbridge Wells) by 5 and 4 in the final. James Henderson, who was a confirmed bachelor but whose heart was clearly melted by her Gallic charm, wrote in the "Newsletter":—

> "She has youth and enthusiasm, is not afflicted with a 'temperament', like others of her race, and looks on life as a joyous adventure. So much has been written about the new champion and her play that there is no need for me to recapitulate biographical and other details. Suffice it to say that she is a new Star in women's golf and that, in spite of the regret which was felt at the passing of yet another championship into foreign hands, her win was most popular. Hers is a charming, unassuming personality. She speaks English far better than the vast majority of the inhabitants of the British Isles, even to the use of idiom, and without the faintest trace of a foreign accent. Small in stature, she is sturdily, though not heavily nor clumsily, built and the strength of her game lies in its consistency with all the clubs. The keynote of her golf, as so it seems, of her life, is its neatness, its polish, its logic, its comprehension of the difficulties of the game, and its avoidance of trouble. We, or some of us, are accustomed to look on the French as an excitable, temperamental race. It is a shallow view, as those who know France well will tell you. The French, or the best of them, are cultured, frugal, mercilessly logical, efficient and disciplined in thought and action. And Mlle. Simone Thion de la Chaume, the new holder of the British Women's Golf championship not only because she was the most consistent golfer in the field, but because of the background of mental and bodily training and of personality which is hers. I think if we look more closely into these matters we shall find more conclusive reasons why we who call ourselves leaders in sport are losing our championships than if we inquire only into our methods of playing our game and pastimes."

1927 British Ladies' Championship.
Miss Enid Wilson and Mlle. C. Blan,
Mlle. Simone de la Chaume (winner) and Miss Dorothy Pearson (runner-up).

Willie Haughton, also inspired, but for a different reason, wrote another poem after witnessing a large and often inexperienced gallery watching the final:

THE GALLERY
(Newcastle, 19th May, 1927)

I.
Woollen legs, silken legs,
Legging it onward,
Tactfully, warily, trudge the twelve hundred;
"Stand! and," as Kelly saith,
"Dare not to draw your breath,"
Then once again down the fairway we thundered.

II.
Hazards to right of us,
Bunkers to left of us,
Stewards in front of us (easily scunnered);
"Keep to the right!" they shout,
"Off the greens! Open out!"
Docile, though much in doubt, move the twelve hundred.

III.
Up go red flags in air;
Stewards turn round and glare,
Wheedling and barging till some of us wondered;
"Oh, but just once to soak
Some of those fussy folk,"
"One on the beak"; and yet none of us blundered,
Not a man lost a stroke, gallant twelve hundred.

IV.
Phalanx'd around each tee,
Standing tip-toe to see
Flappers a-driving where oft we have blundered.
Click! and twelve hundred necks
(Mostly of female sex),
All like one circumflex—
Then we march on, but not *quite* the twelve hundred.

V.
For there be some who feel
T'were for their better weal
To the nineteenth to steal—
These from our ranks for the moment are sundered.
Trudging induces drouth,
Some are not quite in sooth
Just in the prime of youth—
"At the fifteenth we'll rejoin the twelve hundred!"

VI.
Now we're ten holes from home:
Mademoiselle de la Chaume
Standing one up; but our Pearson has blundered!
Playing a "do or die"
(Ours not to reason why)
Out of a hanging lie,
Into the jaws of death goes the ball foundered!

VII.
Pressmen to right of them,
Cam'ras to left of them,
Multitudes cheering them, rightfully honoured;
Pearson and De la Chaume
Carry thier guerdons home,
Say au revoir to the links of Slieve Donard.

VIII.
Ours not to make tirade
Over the game they played:
What impressed *us* was that none of us blundered;
Ours but to gently hint—
This should be noised in print—
"Wisely they trudged and well,
Patient whate'er befell,
"Gallery nonpareil, peerless twelve hundred!"

W. B. H.

High Score The 1928 Open Championship of Ireland attracted a strong and interesting entry, although Walter Hagen "failed to materialise", having been given what the English press described as "an unmerciful hiding" by Archie Compston the previous week at Moor Park. Nevertheless it was an interesting occasion, not only because Ernest Whitcombe, the ultimate winner, established a new course record of 68, but it was noted early on that "Henry Cotton, one of the two English public schoolboy brothers who took up golf as a profession, led the field after the first round with a brilliantly earned 73". A curious feature of the championship was a series of calamitous performances on the 18th hole; one competitor took 12, another 11, and Cotton himself took 9 to return a 75. George Duncan, the holder, was also a casualty and, when asked for an explanation, he stated in some exasperation that it was the most severely bunkered hole in Europe!

Some two weeks after this the members played for the Trigo Trophy for the first time, the fine bronze figure of the Derby winner presented by its owner, and Captain of the Club, William Barnett. His horse had won the Derby, the St. Leger, and Irish St. Leger, all in the same year, and he had commemorated this outstanding success by generous entertainment of the members and caddies alike (many of whom had not unnaturally given the local bookmaker a hard time) and the presentation of fine trophies to the Club and to the Ladies' Club.

The Trigo Trophy

A year later the Irish Professional Championship was visited by 40 m.p.h. gales. One well-known professional took 12 strokes at a par 4 and the popular win of Hughie McNeill from Royal Portrush at the age of 46 was achieved with a four round total of 317, the third highest ever recorded. Drives were often more than halved in length. While one professional holed in one at the 10th his playing partner took 11, and on another occasion one player's ball in flight struck another travelling in the opposite direction; both had hooked their shots on parallel holes. A spectator who had never seen golf played before was assured that this was abnormal.

The great purchase But one event among all others in the 1920s stood out as being possibly the most important in the history of the Club — the purchase of the course. Many years previously Colonel Wallace had carried out negotiations with the Annesley Estate and in 1921, after disagreement on the terms of a new lease, the Club had offered to purchase the land for £4,500. Again a deal could not be struck, and both parties appeared to retreat into a state of frustrated inaction.

Six years later the patient and experienced Stanley Ferguson started the process of securing the long term future of the Club. He first arranged a lease from the Annesley Estate at the nominal rent of 5 shillings a year for the strip of land between the hotel and clubhouse grounds in order to control access to the foreshore. He then put out feelers about purchase, but Lady Mabel was disinclined. At the same time the Finance Committee was warning Council that the Club was spending too much and it was £900 "in the red". Council held an inquest, but made no reductions, and because the Green Committee needed £1,500 a year for maintenance alone, there was talk of increased subscriptions and higher green fees. Harden continued his weeding programme, constructed the 5th green and made more bunkers at the 10th, and while all of this was essential to the well being of the course, the Club needed money and the atmosphere was unsettled. The ladies also wanted the number 2 course extended.

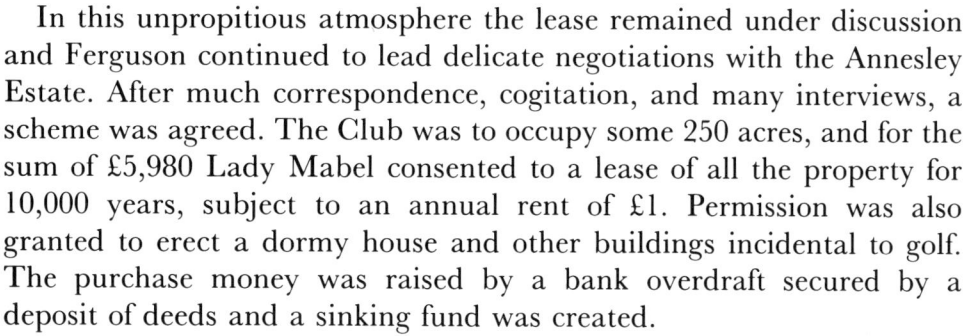

In this unpropitious atmosphere the lease remained under discussion and Ferguson continued to lead delicate negotiations with the Annesley Estate. After much correspondence, cogitation, and many interviews, a scheme was agreed. The Club was to occupy some 250 acres, and for the sum of £5,980 Lady Mabel consented to a lease of all the property for 10,000 years, subject to an annual rent of £1. Permission was also granted to erect a dormy house and other buildings incidental to golf. The purchase money was raised by a bank overdraft secured by a deposit of deeds and a sinking fund was created.

The proposals were approved by Council and unanimously accepted by the Club at a special meeting in 1928. A short while later Council granted a new lease for their club house to the ladies, but not before some further coy enquiries had been received about the timing of an extension to their course from 14 to 18 holes.

It had been a long drawn out affair but Stanley Ferguson's experience and far-sightedness produced an outcome which satisfied all parties and he was subsequently elected an Honorary Life Member in recognition of his outstanding contribution.

*The
 y Mabel Annesley
 Cup*

The Prince, the Record and the Mourne

In 1929 and the early '30s one of the club's main problems was to finance the completion of course developments suggested some years earlier by Colt and to contend, in terms of manpower and cost, with serious problems connected with the course. Fairways, greens and coastal erosion posed diverse challenges; leather jackets had been a constant menace, and winter gales had done serious damage to the sand banks at the first and second holes. In addition there was the cost of buying the lease.

Stanley Ferguson wanted the loan to be reduced and the links to be brought back to first class condition. He felt strongly that deterioration over a period of years had now left it in an embarrassingly poor state and one in which they might not be able to accept championships. He had supporters but Council as a whole felt that members would not respond favourably to an increase in the subscription of 3 guineas. He argued his case vigorously but was opposed by the cautious Willie Haughton and it was to be the spring of 1933 before Ferguson's views prevailed and the membership sanctioned an increase of one guinea and a new entrance fee of ten.

Sincerity and fun

Just before this meeting Haughton died suddenly. He had been ill the previous year but had made a good recovery and was once more active in Club affairs. His passing was a great blow to the Club for few men were better liked. For many years he had given outstanding service and had endeared himself to all by his sincerity and sense of fun. He made a generous bequest to create a staff provident fund, and left part of the residue of his estate to assist in reducing the overdraft.

But back to 1930. In September Bernard Darwin brought the Oxford and Cambridge Golfing Society back to Ireland after a gap of 23 years. In 1907 they had confined their Irish tour to the Dublin area but this time they played Portmarnock first and then came North to Newcastle. The Society won 9-6 but it was a happy reunion for Darwin and his old friend, Guy Ellis. Writing in "The Times" the following week he dwelt on Ellis' former skill but went on to say that the years "may have taken their toll but he is still, however, very cunning. If he cannot get up in

The Oxford and Cambridge Golfing Society versus the Royal County Down Golf Club, 3rd September, 1930.
H. L. H. Greer, E. R. Campbell, J. P. Marston, R. L. Sykes, R. W. Hartley
H. G. B. Ellis, C. Harden, R. H. Oppenheimer, C. B. Mitchell, H. M. Cairnes
J. S. F. Morrison, S. C. Ferguson, N. C. Selway, J. A. Barr, G. P. Jackson, J. B. Johnstone
J. R. Carr, T. J. Ferguson, F. H. Rogers, Bernard Darwin, W. Barnett, D. W. Smyth

two he knows every nook and cranny among the hills to which he can play a strategic stroke. He and his partner (Hardy Greer) won the last hole in a palpitating 7 to give Royal County Down a lead in the morning foursomes."

Darwin's team contained three English internationals, Rex Hartley, Raymond Oppenheimer and J. S. Morrison. It was his first visit to Newcastle and the glorious weather which had attended them at Portmarnock remained. His impressions of both courses, again written in "The Times", are worth recording, and are typical of the great man's writing:—

"To compare two links is always risky; to compare two that have rightly such a good conceit of themselves — one in the South and one in the North — is almost recklessly dangerous. At Newcastle no other course of my acquaintance has any hill so magnificent as Slieve Donard towering above it. To see from one's window its crest just emerging from a great sea of early mist is to taste one of the intenser joys of shaving on the morning of a workless day. Many people know Newcastle, and it is perhaps superfluous to say that it is a course of big and glorious carries, nestling greens, entertainingly blind shots, local knowledge, and beautiful turf ... the kind of golf that people play in their most ecstatic dreams.

Ignorance is often bliss at golf but to be ignorant of Portmarnock and Newcastle is to have missed some of the greatest bliss the game has to give."

The following year the Society came back once more and played the Club during the week preceding the Irish Open Amateur Championship. This time they were drenched to the skin in pitiless rain and both sides were thankful to cancel the afternoon singles and settle for an extended lunch. Most of them stayed to play in the Championship. An excellent week's golf saw E. A. McRuvie (Leven Thistle) beat D. E. B. Soulby from Fortwilliam on the 31st green in the

Looking back up the 3rd hole from the sandhills.

Looking southward from the hill at the 11th towards the short 10th.

final. Darwin himself played and, unlike today, his literary contributions to "The Times" were anonymous, merely headed "from our golf correspondent". His love of the amateur game and his intense enjoyment of its triumphs and tragedies were never more simply revealed than when he wrote:

> *"This championship has provided some surprising things, as there always are, and some good matches. Yet it is the illustrious obscure who always provide the best fun and I derived more pleasure from two players whose blushes may be spared than from the potential champions. They halved the 18th in six, with a favouring wind, and followed this by halving the nineteenth in seven, in both cases without touching sand. This is the kind of thing that has made Britons what they are and had I at my disposal the ample spaces of a three-volume novel I would write only of them. As it is I must unwillingly descant on those who are quite erroneously deemed of greater public interest."*

His own progress in the championship was not inconsiderable and he described it as having

> *"unobtrusively scuffled his way through to the fifth round where a cataclysmic top into the pond at the 17th, followed by a rather inglorious half at the 18th, finished a good struggle against Soulby."*

During the next two years the condition of the course deteriorated and further serious coastal erosion took place. The Board of Greenkeeping Research offered the consoling view that the greens would grow again when the depredations of the leather jackets ceased. Adding to the tribulations of the green committee was a plague of weeds, presumably thriving in grass badly affected by pests, and in desperation they were treated with paraffin and petrol. It is not recorded if this startling move was efficacious but we must presume not for there was a severe shortage of caddies caused by their absence on weeding activities and Council instructed the Green Committee to use women and children for this work instead.

"... one of the horses could be done away with".

These efforts slowly prevailed and a confident step into the 20th Century was taken when a tractor and mowing machine were bought "the cost not to exceed £300". The minutes record, nevertheless, that "one of the horses could be done away with".

THE PRINCE

The Autumn of 1932 saw Wilson Smyth installed as President of the Golfing Union of Ireland and a visit from the Prince of Wales in November caused something of a local stir. His party included the Home Secretary (The Rt. Hon. Sir John Gilmour) the Comptroller to the Prince of Wales (Admiral Sir Lionel Halsey) and Equerries Major Aird, Mr. F. A. Newsome and Lieut. C. A. R. Shillington. In a game which he clearly enjoyed, he partnered Wilson Smyth against the Hon. Harry Mulholland and Major Hammond-Smith, "judging his 20 foot putt to a nicety on the 18th green to win the match. More than a hundred people cheered heartily at the Prince's victory."

H.R.H. The Prince of Wales and Wilson Smyth, with Fred Rogers and Willie Haughton spectating.

So much had he enjoyed his round that he unceremoniously cut short a visit the following morning to Barbour's Mill at Hilden and headed once more on an unplanned visit to Newcastle, this time playing with the then Attorney General, The Rt. Hon. A. B. Babington.

Party piece   Towards the end of the year, Alex Robertson ended his engagement as professional and there were no fewer than 146 applications for the vacancy. A sub committee produced a short list but recommended only one name to Council, Jimmy Adams of Kilmarnock. He was a player of substantial ability and, although only 22 years old, had an excellent reputation for teaching. His nomination was accepted without any further reference to the list of applicants at "£2 a week retaining fee, with a free workshop, water and electricity and with the sole right to sell clubs, balls and other requisites."

He remained with the club only two years but his "party piece" was talked about years later. Whether for fun or a wager, he was able to stand at the top of the ninth hill and hit balls onto the green. He was succeeded in 1935 by Jack MacLachlan of Barrassie who remained with the club until 1955 as a popular, diligent and successful club professional.

Council, conscious of the fact that in the long dark evenings the staff "had little or nothing to do", bought a wireless for their use but, not unmindful of the members, bought a portable one which "would be available for use in the Club for the purpose of listening in to cricket, football, or other sport which might be of interest to them".

The tradition of caddies' dinners, which had been continuing since the very early days, was still strong. They often attracted over 100 in number and were preceded by a lunch for the officers of the Club and Council who were later to wait at table upon the caddies.

Caddies fees in 1933 were:—

9 holes 1s.2d.   27 holes 2s.6d.
18 holes 1s.8d. 36 holes 3s.2d.

but they were still not employed on Sundays, nor were they for some years to come.

"...the officers of the Club waited at table upon the caddies".

With some improvement in the condition of the course at the end of 1932, Council acceded to a request from the Irish Ladies Golfing Union to hold their championship in 1933 and also decided to accept what came to be known as the Home Internationals, the first international matches having been played the previous year at Troon. The original choice of venue had been Royal Portrush who were unable to accept because the course, at that time, was undergoing its great reconstruction. Not content with this, the Club housed the Irish Open Amateur again in September, the final of which was notable for Eric Fiddian's feat of holing in one twice and still losing on the 34th green to Jack McLean, the 22 year old Scottish holder of both his native and Irish championships.

The next two years were comparatively uneventful and 1935 saw the Ladies Golf Union bringing their championship back to Newcastle, Miss Wanda Morgan beating Miss Pam Barton by 3 and 2 in the 36 hole final of a most successful event. Immediately prior to the championship a strong Scottish side won the Home Internationals in which Ireland scored a notable victory over England, the first time they had done so since 1909. Ireland's team included two Royal County Down players, Daisy Ferguson, daughter of Stanley Ferguson, and Betty Ellis, daughter of H. G. B. Ellis. A month later Miss Ferguson beat Miss Ellis in the final of the Irish Ladies Championship at Rosapenna and Council decided to acknowledge their successful performance by having a celebratory lunch in the Clubhouse to which the Council of the Ladies Club were invited and at which the Misses Ferguson and Ellis were guests of honour.

The Recorder of Belfast, Judge Herbert Thompson, who was Captain of the Club at the time, did much to make the event a most successful occasion as he did later in the year at a complimentary dinner in Belfast to Fred Rogers on his retirement after 11 years as a strong and popular Honorary Secretary. The Recorder would not have admitted to being one of the most outstanding golfers in the Province but he was acknowledged to be one of the most witty after-dinner speakers of his time.

In the earlier part of 1936 the state of the course had been continuing to cause concern and there was still much anxiety over coast erosion along the first and second fairways. Economies in running the Clubhouse were sought and Stanley Ferguson and J. E. Wilson reiterated their view that the annual subscription was far too low. Eventually Council decided to take a major step forward and the appointment of the Club's first salaried secretary saw the arrival from Ferndown, Dorset, of Captain Kenneth Burrell. Within two months he had produced a management plan which was accepted in full by Council and he was given full responsibility for course, catering and clubhouse upkeep.

Salaried Secretary

In the summer of that year, the Green Committee erected three groynes on the beach, using 200 railway sleepers, in an attempt to stem the lateral movement of sand. This proved helpful in combating erosion, and more were authorised the next year.

Miss Wanda Morgan receiving the 1935 British Ladies' Championship Trophy.

"a request for the Hotel Quintet to play on the No. 2 Course".

On a lighter note, a request was granted for the Hotel Quintet "to play on the No. 2 course during the summer" free of charge. A musical director, who was to be with them in connection with broadcasting, was allowed free golf on No. 1 course and the B.B.C. official who was to accompany him was required to pay the usual fee. Fine distinctions.

In the year or two leading up to 1938 much discussion had taken place on the inadequacy of clubhouse facilities, and the Annual General Meeting of that year approved plans for better accommodation, particularly for visitors. The scheme was deferred because of the Munich crisis but it is interesting to note that the Council's thinking behind it was virtually identical to that which prompted the major extension exactly 50 years later at the time of the Club's Centenary. The extension then was to provide almost the same facilities as today although all at ground floor level. At the Annual Meeting which passed the plans Mr. Saxton J. Payne, one of the old guard, stated that he would be sorry to see the characteristics of the Clubhouse altered in any way, but in a vision of the future he went on to suggest that an "air landing ground" should be provided for it would certainly be needed in the years ahead.

"Dullest on record"

The Irish Open Amateur came back to Newcastle again in 1938 and was described by one eminent correspondent as "the dullest on record". This may have been partly true of the earlier rounds but there was some great golf in the later stages, particularly from Dr. McCallum, the Scottish international, and two great Irish players of the day, James Mahon and James Bruen.

McCallum's best golf came in the third round when he went out in 33 against H. Nicholson of Fairhaven, winning every hole. The "Irish Times" recorded that "the match came to an abrupt end at the tenth". It had been a wonderful year for the legendary Bruen, then still only 18 years old. He had been leader of the Walker Cup team at St. Andrews, winner of the Irish Close and Open Amateur Championships, and probably the only amateur on this side of the Atlantic with a handicap of plus 4, and more often than not playing to it.

The 36 hole final saw Bruen equalling Lionel Munn's achievement in winning both the Irish Amateur Close and Open championships in the same year, and with his score at level fours when the match finished he beat the unfortunate Mahon by 9 and 8. It was a decisive triumph, but few amateurs in the country, with the possible exception of John Burke or Dr. Billy O'Sullivan, would have done much better. During the championship Bruen had the oldest and most experienced of the Newcastle caddies, Hughie Bannon, who knew every blade of grass on the links and who still, given the slightest opportunity, regaled his employers with stories of the time he had caddied for the Prince of Wales six years earlier.

Nearly complete

It is, perhaps, not inappropriate at this time to record the lengths of the individual holes as they were at this time. The standard scratch was 74, the total length 6,690 yards and the course had, with the exception of the twelfth and fifteenth greens which were each shortly to be moved back some thirty or forty yards, finally acquired the general layout we know today.

1	512 yards	10	200 yards
2	376 yards	11	443 yards
3	450 yards	12	441 yards
4	160 yards	13	434 yards
5	440 yards	14	205 yards
6	394 yards	15	407 yards
7	136 yards	16	238 yards
8	426 yards	17	397 yards
9	488 yards	18	543 yards

Bruen returned in 1939 to play in the Irish Open Championship and marked the occasion by creating a new course record in the first round with a very fine 66, a feat unchallenged for 29 years, and a score in which he also three putted twice and narrowly missed his birdie on the 18th. He was now at the peak of his meteoric career and was the most exciting of players to watch — the famous loop at the top of his backswing, his prodigious length, and gloriously delicate short game, all created what became a legend in Irish golf. After the first round, the "Belfast Newsletter" noted

James Bruen at the top of the famous "Bruen loop."

"Among the 72's is the first of the Ulster competitors, Fred Daly, formerly of Lurgan and now of City of Derry. A. D. Locke (South Africa), one of the younger school from which much is expected, took 73, misjudging a number of short approaches".

The championship was won by Arthur Lees with a four round total of 287".

Wartime economies

The Club's 50th year opened in the shadow of impending war and with the loan account at £3,000, but to celebrate the anniversary the new lounge was opened, a special competition was held, and 50 members attended the Golden Jubilee Dinner. It was a happy choice that Fred Rogers' brother, Sidney, had been elected Captain in May, for in September war was declared and he was to remain in office for the next four years. Council, with only eight attending, moved rapidly to meet new circumstances; competitions were cancelled, work on the shore banks was discontinued, both indoor and outdoor staff were cut to a basic minimum and the caddie master's services were dispensed with. Economies were effected throughout the Clubhouse, periodicals reduced, and the telephone in the Council Room was shared with the air raid precautions authorities. The annual report was not circulated to members and was displayed instead on the Notice Board. Nevertheless, certain priorities were deemed essential; the professional was to remain and a caddies competition and dinner was once more held in 1940.

The war years were even more difficult than in 1914-18, and the monthly accounts were consistently showing losses. Some Council meetings were held in Belfast and frequently were not held at all. There were many resignations, only the minimum of maintenance to the course was carried out, and sheep grazed on the course throughout the year.

Towards the end of 1943 Stanley Ferguson, the first of four successive generations of Stanley Ferguson to be members, died. The tribute from the Club, which he had joined in 1891, was well deserved:

"His sound judgment and wise outlook on all matters was recognised by his colleagues. When negotiations for the purchase of the links broke down in 1927, Mr. Ferguson pointed out what it would mean if this opportunity were missed, and it is entirely due to his personal effort that the Club owns the links today."

Stanley Ferguson.

The difficulties which war posed the Club were very great. Eighty four members were serving in the Forces and the annual meeting of 1944 was attended by only 16 people.

Money was needed badly and subscriptions were raised from 4 to 6 guineas. The foreshore at the first and second holes had been riven by gales and the Clubhouse was in bad shape. Despite the fact that only the most essential maintenance could be done on course or buildings for the duration, the Club, although shaken, was never subdued, and in June 1945 victory in Europe was marked by raising the price of wines and spirits by 3d a half glass, a decision received with dismay by the members and hotly debated by Council for many months.

The Mourne

There was, however, one very significant move which took place in the closing years of the war. Gerald Annesley, grandson of the first president and now landlord, took a positive step forward on behalf of the townspeople of Newcastle. He wrote to Council reminding them that the town had become a substantial seaside resort, and was no longer the fishing village of 1889. He proposed the establishment of a club for residents of the Newcastle area, under the auspices of Royal County Down, and with separate premises. Council's characteristic reaction was to appoint a sub-committee; this did not betoken reluctance but they wished to be sure of the implications for all parties. For example, on handicapping and other issues the Golfing Union of Ireland had to be consulted.

Two years later details were finalised, but in the meantime Mourne Golf Club, as it had been named, was seeking accommodation, and the huts which had been used by the Civil Defence Authorities between the Clubhouse and Slieve Donard Hotel were found suitable. A lease was arranged as soon as the Government sold them. Hours were set during which their members should play and financial relations, membership control and oversight of their rules were agreed. Mourne would fix its own subscriptions and handicaps and be affiliated to the Golfing Union of Ireland. Thus was established what quickly became a thriving club and a major contributor to the golfing scene in Ulster. Mourne made a generous and complimentary gesture to Royal County Down by electing Gerald Annesley and Wilson Smyth Honorary Life Members.

The Veterans' Cup

Whiskey for sale and an Airborne Kilt

With the end of World War II in 1945 the Club, like the nation, faced a formidable task. Six years of austerity had left it lean and undernourished, and eleven names had been added to the Roll of Honour. The years ahead were to be uphill, with severe claims on resources from both course and clubhouse. Competitions were still suspended and food and drink were scarce.

By 1947 the overdraft had risen to £7,000 and the Annual Report warned that a six guinea subscription was not enough. Weeks later Council approved the rise in principle, but raised the price of drinks as an interim measure to condition the membership to what might lie ahead, although two years passed before the increase was accepted.

The Ladies were also feeling the pinch but handsomely increased their annual contribution from £50 to £200. Council gratefully acknowledged this gesture and reciprocated by allowing the ladies to use part of the men's clubhouse but only if accompanied by Club members. A threatening footnote to this concession stated that "no Scotch Whisky will be served".

Austerity continued and a dire state of affairs was confirmed later in the year when Council decided that "about 600 bottles of Irish Whiskey redundant in stock, at present lying in Belfast, should be sold at 54s.0d a bottle approximately". A sub committee of senior Council members, appropriate to the gravity of such a decision, was empowered to dispose of it "at the most advantageous price".

Cecil Ewing and J. B. Carr.
Irish Open Amateur Final, 1948.

Despite these problems work on the course had been gathering momentum; protection of the shore banks had restarted and fertilisers were becoming available again. In these circumstances Council felt able to accept the first championship since 1939, and September of 1948 saw the return of the Irish Open Amateur when Cecil Ewing (Co. Sligo) beat J. B. Carr by one hole in a somewhat undistinguished final, thus reversing a previous year's result when Carr had beaten Ewing on the latter's home course, Rosses Point, in the final of "The West."

October saw a resumption of "winter work". The 12th fairway was widened, a new championship tee at the 15th was constructed, and new bunkers created at the 14th. The life blood of the Club was beginning to flow again and Gerald Annesley selected a 60 foot tree from part of his estate at Castlewellan to provide a new flagpole. Its removal to Newcastle provided an intriguing problem for tractors, escorts and outriders on a road not so straight as it is now. When it finally arrived at the Clubhouse, Mr. Gould, the carpenter from King Street, was summoned to remove the top 20 feet to provide a yardarm. Those in charge reflected afterwards that the journey might have been less hazardous had Mr. Gould been invited to perform his task before the tree left Clanvaraghan.

A pole too long

A special meeting early in 1949 finally agreed to increase the subscription to 10 guineas, and two new classes of member were created to encourage the young — Juveniles (16-21) and Juniors (21-30). The Club benefited from a gratifying increase in youthful and enthusiastic players, many of them sons of members, and in 1956 the Annual Report recorded that one of them, Harry McCaw, had won five of the major club competitions. He reports to his co-author a little unease in certain quarters at the time but he was invited the same year to serve on Council to represent the views of the younger element, a state of bliss from which he had not emerged some 30 years later.

Nevertheless, the financial position of the Club was still bad. Life membership was abolished, the cost of afternoon tea was increased from 9d to one shilling and a reduction was made in the size of helpings at luncheon. The Captain, Major Charles Davies, invited the members to offer suggestions for a long term management plan, but no flash of brilliance emerged and the membership left the affairs of the Club in the hands of Council who, among many other important decisions, recorded one which still stands today; namely that if a member achieves a hole in one "he was not to stand treat to the whole club without special permission". Thus one of the legendary penalties of the game became conditional.

a reduction made in size of helpings ..."

In December 1949 the members were instructed, when not playing in competitions, to tee the ball up through the green. The course was not in good order but the decision, regarded by many as humiliating on a links, was in a good cause for the Club was to house the Ladies Championship again in 1950 after a gap of 15 years. As on its five previous visits to Newcastle, it once more proved a delightful event to host and produced some fine golf, particularly from the ultimate winner, the Vicomtesse de Saint Sauveur who, during the week, relentlessly worked her way through an impressive array of international class victims, finally disposing of that most experienced of Scottish players, Mrs. Jessie Valentine. The Vicomtesse was a popular winner and the combination of her attractive appearance and golfing ability set many an old golfing heart gently aflutter.

The Vicomtesse de Saint Sauveur

Social changes in golf arose because of economic stresses. Caddies had been in erratic supply since 1918 and, after the second world war, the acuteness of the problem was partly relieved by caddie-cars. Henderson wrote in his earlier history that "they are now quite commonplace on all courses and need no description". They became so popular at Newcastle in the early days that a rent of 10s0d per annum had to be charged to store them, but they never acquired a popularity with the more traditionally minded. Henderson was surely one of these for he wrote "I am glad my golfing days were over before I was forced to drag my clubs behind me on a steel chariot mounted on rubber wheels".

The late 40's and early 50's had been years of recovery but 1952 saw a setback in the resignation through illness of the Secretary, Captain Kenneth Burrell. He was elected an honorary member, a compliment also paid to him by the Mourne Golf Club, and was succeeded in office shortly afterwards by Squadron Leader Robert Taylor of Bolton. Taylor had a distinguished war record, flying the notoriously hazardous unarmed pathfinder missions over Germany. He was shot down,

Jessie Valentine (left) and the Vicomtesse de Saint Sauveur.

imprisoned, and escaped with the aid of the French Resistance to return to Coastal Command and the award of a D.F.C. for outstanding bravery. His organisational talents were not lost on the Club and it was but a short time before he had made significant changes in the style of management.

A giant goes

The death of Wilson Smyth in 1953 removed a remarkable figure from the life of the Club. In his own way he had been as much a character as George Combe and his two great predecessors in the office of Honorary Secretary, Fred Hoey and Fred Rogers. Captain in 1921, 1931 and 1945, and Honorary Secretary for the 17 years before his death, his contribution to the whole life of the Club was substantial. Some occasionally thought him autocratic but few golf clubs are successfully run without just a touch of it here and there and the tribute paid to him by Council on September 26, 1953, perfectly summed up the feelings of his fellow members:—

"A man of transparent honesty of purpose and action, a staunch and loyal friend in any emergency, his broad humanity has been an inspiration to all who knew him. His outstanding characteristic was his integrity".

Wilson Smyth.

Royal Patron

The duties of Honorary Secretary which he had performed for so long were undertaken by Stanley Ferguson (Junior) until 1956 when he relinquished them in favour of William Smyth, a son of Wilson. Willie had grown up in a family steeped in the game, and his affection for the Club and great knowledge of the course fitted him well for the office which he was to hold so ably for the next twentyone years.

A further mark of Royal favour came in 1953 when the Duke of Edinburgh became Patron, but even this graciousness could not reduce the bank overdraft which had shown little sign of decreasing since its creation 25 years earlier on the purchase of the links from the Annesley Estate. Membership had fallen, and the need for new course equipment did not help matters. Economies in Clubhouse and course staff were made, and a heartening increase in green fee revenue in 1954 encouraged Council to produce a club tie for the first time.

The same year saw the death of a distinguished life member, H. M. Cairnes. A product of Portmarnock, where he was almost a potentate, Cairnes had been a comparative latecomer to golf, for he devoted most of his spare time as a young man to riding, becoming what was known then as a "gentleman jockey", but when he took up golf he mastered a fine technique quickly and reached the final of the Close Championship in 1906, winning it the following year. He also reached the final of the Irish Open Amateur in 1908, a considerable feat in those days because it was a highly regarded tournament attracting entries from the best golfers in Britain. He played at Newcastle often in his later years and was still a scratch golfer at the age of 70. He and Wilson Smyth were close friends and did much between them to foster especially friendly contacts between Royal County Down and Portmarnock, of which latter club he was captain on several occasions and president for some years before his death.

The success with which a club tie was greeted by members

Stanley Ferguson junior.

prompted the creation of a blazer badge and the design of both has remained unaltered. Blazers are not now part of actual golfing attire but in the early days there were few who did not wear a red jacket. 'Those worn at Royal County Down were red with a green collar, and the only one known to be in existence, worn originally by Thomas Dickson, winner of the first Irish Close Championship in 1893 and Captain in 1894, was kindly given back to the Club by his family in 1988.

In his earlier writings about the Club James Henderson said he well remembered Fred Rogers, Fred Hoey and George Combe playing so clad, and that Harold Reade would certainly have regarded himself as improperly dressed had he not done so. In wild weather some sort of rainproof affair was donned with suitable apologetic explanations.

Henderson recalled that George Combe possessed a waterproof kilt which he frequently wore over his trousers while shooting and on the day of the 1913 Scratch medal he was induced to borrow it as protection from the violence of the weather. The rain lashed in almost horizontal torrents in a south easterly gale and the morning had seen Lord Glerawley returning to the Clubhouse with a score well up the nineties and so benumbed with cold that the dressing room boy had to disrobe him. Despite this forbidding example, and encouraged by a good lunch and Combe's kilt, Henderson sallied forth to the first tee. Combe accompanied him to see how he fared and was just in time to see the kilt suddenly ballooning upwards on his backswing, rendering Henderson momentarily airborne and giving a new and more literal meaning to the air shot.

Henderson counted a penalty shot, removed the offending garment and went on to win the medal with a 93, the third highest score recorded in that competition. The highest had been 101 in 1898 but with a guttie ball.

"... giving a new and more literal meaning to the airshot".

But back to contemporary time. 1955 opened agreeably with the reduction in the price of port to 2s6d a glass and the news that the Mourne Club wished to extend their lease. September saw a most successful Irish Open Amateur Championship, the second major men's event since the war and won by John Fitzgibbon of Cork who beat J. W. Hulme of Warrenpoint in the final, and at the end of the year news reached Council that the Ladies' Club was becoming so popular that they wished to increase their membership ceiling from 250 to 300. The men's club happily acceded, but the new figure was to include "military and colonial members".

The Oxford and Cambridge Golfing Society team against the Club in August 1956.
Insets: R. W. Hutchinson (Capt. R.C.D.G.C.), J. A. Barr
Back row: W. A. McNeill, P. G. Shillington, Dr J. M. Barbour, Dr D. M. Marsh, A. Douglas, G. H. Foster
2nd row: H. E. Impey, I. H. McCaw, R. O'Brien, G. H. Micklem, R. A. Speedy, M. Grindrod
3rd row: J. J. J. Johnston, A. E. Shepperson, V. N. Hogg, R. T. Gardiner-Hill, S. K. Lockhart
Front row: W. H. Whitelaw, Wm Smyth, A. D. Cave, S. C. Ferguson, J. G. Blackwell

The following year was comparatively uneventful, although it did see the welcome return of the Oxford and Cambridge Golfing Society in August. Gerald Micklem captained an impressive line-up which included Alan Cave, John Blackwell and Willie Whitelaw (all four of whom were later to Captain the R. & A) and several English internationals and Walker Cup players including Alec Shepperson and David Marsh. It is perhaps not surprising that the combined golfing talents of the County Down team were unequal to the task, and they succumbed 9 matches to 3. Nevertheless it was a golfing occasion to remember and resulted in many long standing friendships renewed over the years at Newcastle, Rye and St. Andrews.

The match was a pleasing prelude to the end of a year which saw the Club on a sound financial footing and able to look to the future with confidence.

Piped Water and Shifting Sand

August 1956 had seen the resignation of Robert Taylor as Club Secretary and on January 1, 1957, Squadron Leader Arthur C. Jones was appointed to succeed him. A man of single mindedness and great gentility, he was to become one of the outstanding golf club secretaries of his day and over the next 20 years ran the Club's affairs with clinical efficiency and great courtesy.

Nearly a quarter of a century had passed since the Home Internationals had been played at Newcastle, and more extensive organisation was required for spectators and visitors. The Club was just on its feet again for the post-war travails had had far reaching effects. A professional agronomist from England was helping the splendid Bridges (seconded with the kind agreement of Malone Golf Club) and the links were in fine trim. Council thought that to use the championship tees would not be inappropriate but after the first practice day in a severe wind the team captains were unanimous in their view that those at the 2nd and 9th were too difficult, and so the medal tees were substituted.

Leonard Crawley wrote:—

"England won the Raymond Trophy and the mythical triple crown in the Home International matches, beating Scotland by twelve matches to three, Wales by nine matches to six and Ireland by ten and a half to four and a half.

Only one member of the English side is over thirty years old, and it would therefore be correct to refer to these young men as the best young International side within living memory. Only the old gentlemen who persist in selecting the week of the equinox for the International matches could be criticised. The English Selection Committee has dispensed with many of the old boiling fowls who have held their team together for so long. Every member of the young English side has distinguished himself in stroke play and every member of the side has a first class method".

Praising Gerald Micklem, he went on:—

"They were found, encouraged taught and produced by men who know the game. What frankly surprised me is that they have won the Championship in only two years. Even such fine golfers as J. B. Carr and David Blair have taken their time to emerge. It is of interest that Michael Bonallack, playing for England for the first time, was the only one left with one match to play on the final day and the chance of a grand slam. It matters not that he lost to Peter Froggatt (later Vice-Chancellor of Queen's University, Belfast) of Ireland on the last afternoon and he had to be content with five wins and one defeat."

Although Ireland performed poorly there was consolation when a large crowd saw Joe Carr demolish Scotland's amateur champion, Reid Jack. Sitting disconsolately in the locker room afterwards a bewildered Jack remarked to Arthur Jones: "I haven't got over it yet — two over fours and beaten six and five!". Carr started with an eagle at the first and was five under par for the 13 holes played. The following afternoon he had lost some of his touch against Guy Wolstenholme of England who won by 6 and 4 although having been beaten by Reid Jack in his match against Scotland.

All this was amateur golf at its best; brilliant and exciting play at one moment and followed in the next by displays of golfing frailty with which we can all equate.

It was a most successful event and Darwin was complimentary:—

Joe Carr and Reid Jack.

"I am ashamed to say that I had not recognised Royal County Down as one of the world's greatest seaside courses. I now say that I have seen nothing finer, either as a test of the game or from the point of scenic splendour."

He concluded his final report on the internationals asking: "is Newcastle the greatest course in the world?" Like "jesting Pilate", he did not stay for an answer but went on his way, leaving the members of the club with the comfortable feeling that they had been handsomely done by.

In 1956 Mrs. Zara Bolton of Royal Portrush had captained the successful British Isles Curtis Cup team which won at Prince's, Sandwich, and 1958 saw an interesting sequel when Miss Daisy Ferguson of the Royal County Down Ladies Club retained the captaincy for Ireland. Competing at Brae Burn, Massachusetts, she successfully led her team to a halved match, thus keeping the cup and becoming the first British captain ever to bring back an international golf trophy from

Daisy Ferguson with the Wallace Williamson Cup, (v Belgium) the Curtis Cup, (v U.S.A.) and the Vagliano trophy (v France) all won by the British Isles Team and held by the Royal County Down Golf Club during 1957, 1958 and 1959.

the United States, a feat not equalled for another 28 years when Great Britain and Ireland won the Curtis Cup 13-5 at Prairie Dunes, Kansas. To mark the occasion the Club held a cocktail party at which the Curtis Cup was taken into safe keeping and Miss Ferguson was presented with a commemorative silver salver.

The following year saw two interesting events at Newcastle, the visit of the Commonwealth Ladies Teams and the last of the Irish Open Amateurs. In the former, teams from Australia, Canada, New Zealand and South Africa joined some prominent Irish players following the Commonwealth Team Championship which had taken place at St. Andrews the previous week. It was a happy occasion and some days of practice were followed by a stroke competition won by Joan Fletcher of Australia. There was an abundance of golfing talent, but it was only natural that the attention focused on Mrs. Marlene Streit. This engaging and diminutive 25 year old Canadian, only four feet eleven inches tall, already held the British and American Ladies Amateur Championships, and had won the Canadian Open six times and the Canadian Close seven times, the first of which when only 17. At Newcastle she was runner up to Miss Fletcher but was undoubtedly the best lady amateur in the world at that time and delighted her admiring spectators during the week with some scintillating play.

Late hour? The night before the stroke competition, the Irish Ladies Golf Union gave a cocktail party in the Clubhouse to which some of the younger members were invited to provide, as Arthur Jones quaintly put it, "company of a contemporary nature" for some of the lady visitors. Next morning one or two harassed team captains expressed concern at the late hour at which some of their charges had returned to their hotels.

The last Irish Open Amateur took place later in the year, although the fact that it was to be discontinued was not known at the time. Dry weather had parched the greens and high winds over the first two days made good scoring a nightmare.

Eventually John Duncan of Shandon Park ran out the winner with a four round total of 313, beating

John Duncan (right) receiving the Championship Trophy from Dr. Billy O'Sullivan, President of the Golfing Union of Ireland.

THE SHORE DEFENCES
"...more than 3,000 sleepers were placed by the green staff in 431 man days."

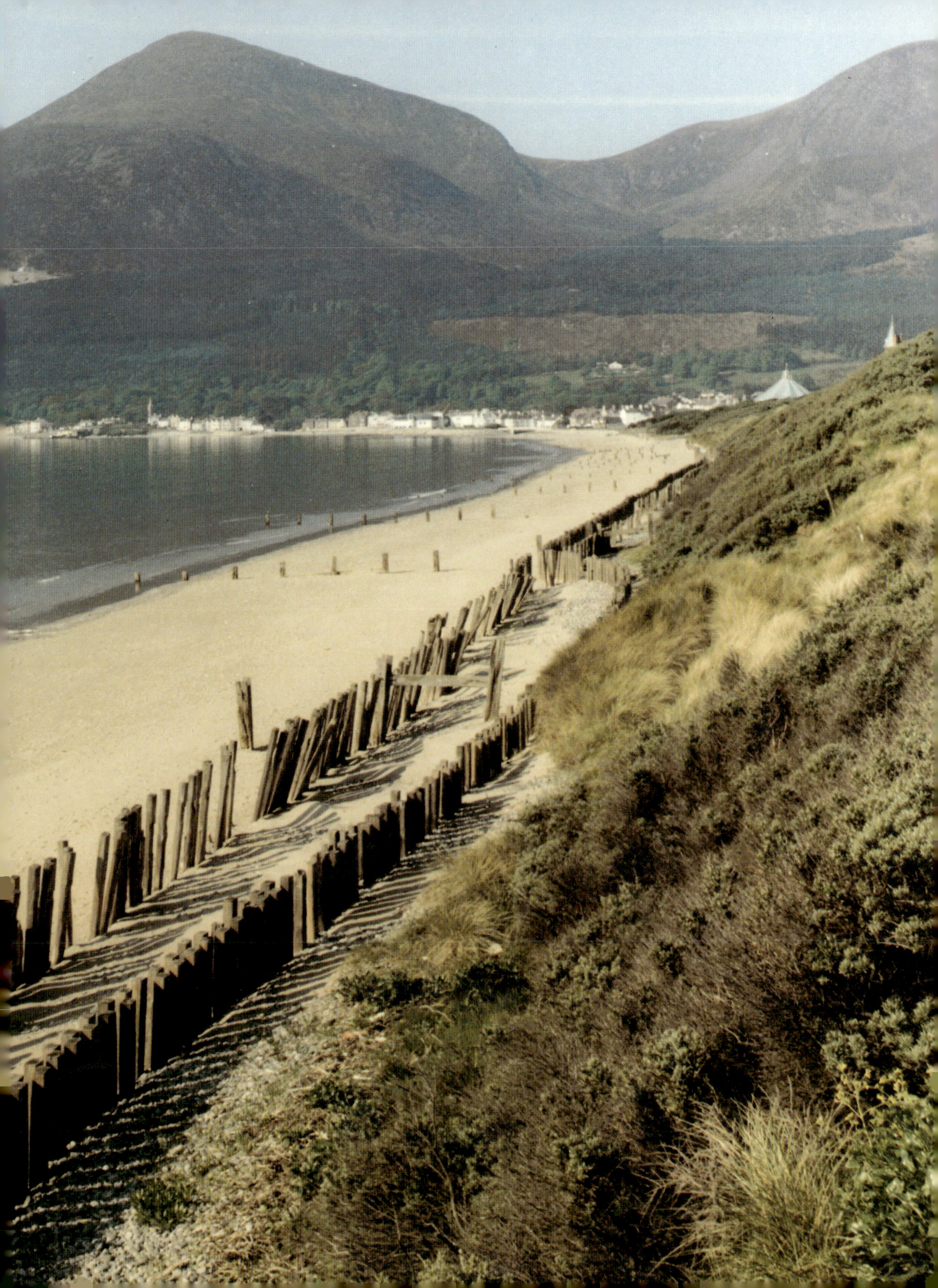

Graham Gordon of Troon St. Meddans by five clear shots. Throughout the event putting had been exceedingly difficult on glassy greens and there were many tales of woe in the Clubhouse. One player, for instance, about to putt from four feet on the seventh green, watched in dismay as his ball was blown ten feet away. Not unnaturally this give rise to renewed talk of a proper watering system.

A midnight find

But to digress, Arthur Jones, a Secretary dry in wit if not in conviviality, wrote in the December edition of Golf Illustrated about an interesting recent experience:—

> *"I returned to the Club rather late the other evening to be greeted with the news that water was leaking from the attic. I watched the drops falling persistently to the floor and, while recognising my duty to investigate, I was uneasily aware that to gain access to the storage tanks among the rafters required a feat of some agility in a man half my age. Moreover, it was a Saturday night and I had returned to the Club after being a guest at dinner of a visiting Golfing Society. It was not an auspicious moment.*
>
> *On the fifth trip into the rafters my conviction that the damage was in a completely inaccessible spot did nothing to improve my temper and when, crawling backwards in a confined space between tanks and wall I encountered an obstruction, I cast it roughly behind me. Emerging from the rafters I saw the obstruction to be a long thin book. I brought it down with me. It was the Club's bar stock book for 1900, and the following afternoon I sat down to examine it.*
>
> *The entries were penned in careful copperplate showing cost and selling prices, and also stock details. Interest carried me back to an age before my time ... the best Bavarian Lager and Pilsner beers at 2s.2d per dozen half-pints, carriage free all the way from Munich. There, written on the thinnest of paper, in beautiful copperplate, and couched in the dignified language of that time, a testimonial from the Forth Corinthian Yacht Club for a man who was to become a well-known steward at Newcastle. In those days members paid 2s.0d. for a bottle of claret, 6d for liqueurs and brandy, and 3d and 6d for cigars, though strangely enough there is an item for cigarettes costing 7s.6d per 100 and selling at 1d each.*
>
> *But it was whiskey that kept the bar going, and consumption of other beverages was relatively small. One drank glasses of whiskey in those days at 6d a glass, and in Ireland a glass of whiskey is just about one-tenth of a bottle. Only Irish whiskey was listed, one by one, by those then famous brands, and for 33 consecutive months a contemptuous tick was marked against the item "Whisky, Scotch" to show nil stock.*
>
> *The Irish Amateur Open Championship was played at the Club that September and there was a substantial English and Scottish entry, but though the bar sales were high no Scotch Whisky was stocked (how different now!). That same month appeared a note that 64 glasses of whiskey were sold at cost price. Could that have been to the winner, Harold Hilton of Royal Liverpool, the more economically to fill that huge championship cup? Gross bar profit for a full calendar year was £118.10.5½d.*
>
> *Fading daylight brought me back to the present and I went up to the bar. As I paid 5s.0d for a glass of whiskey I had the compensation of knowing that though the cost of refreshment had increased tenfold during the last 60 years, the Club's income from bar profits had increased by a substantially greater proportion."*

But back to the course. The trying conditions in the 1959 Irish Open Amateur resulted in veiled criticism and generated much discussion on the pros and cons of a watering system. Opinion was divided, with the

The Barbour Cup

Storm warning

more traditionally-minded members maintaining that golfers should adapt to the elements, but more modern thinking prevailed in the best interests of the course. Architect father and son members, George and Brian Hobart, made recommendations on water pressures and runs of piping and in 1960 the scheme was completed in 41 man days by the Club's own staff at the remarkably low cost of £900.

While the system was basically good, it required too much manual handling, and with added periodical movement of pipes and sprinklers the thinking turned to an automatic programmed system which could be operated at night, so avoiding evaporation and interference with play, but it was not until 1972 that a £13,000 system covering both courses and some tees was installed by a specialist.

Early in 1961 concern was expressed at the arrival of a caravan park close to the Club's northern boundary. Between this and the course lay some 8 acres of land which the Club had tried to buy over the years. It was owned by members of a local family, some living in the Newcastle area and some further afield. Protracted negotiations could not find agreement among the family, never mind with the Club, and it was finally purchased nearly 20 years later by the owner of the caravan park for more than £20,000, with the Club retaining a 50 foot wide strip for protection.

In 1962 the Ladies' Club were revising their rules and inquired if Royal County Down had any suggested amendments. This allowed the opportunity to suggest the repeal of the draconian, long-outdated provision (on which they had insisted at the turn of the Century) that ladies on the Number 1 Course should allow men to pass them on all occasions.

Erosion continued to be a worrying problem. For many years the sandbanks above high water mark had been vulnerable to wind and high seas and in 1938, after expert examination, additional groynes were erected. These were effective to a degree but by 1960 deterioration had naturally taken place and approaches were made to the Government to help with costly sea defences. These were abortive and erosion continued, albeit on a limited scale, until the advent of a fierce four day storm which raged from October 22 to 25, 1961. Arthur Jones recorded that some three years previously he had placed markers on the vulnerable area just North of the third tees to measure ground loss along the top of the sand bank, but:

"On October 24, at the height of the storm, I stood by those markers helplessly watching the sea below crash into the foot of the sandbanks, removing tons of sand at a time. All the brushwood laid as a protection against wind erosion had already gone. As I watched, the top of the sandbank began to subside, falling into the cavities below, and I was reminded of the relative impotence of man in his fight against the fury of the sea. Within two hours the markers had been washed away and the end of the storm on October 25 saw 18 feet of land lost to the sea since I had originally positioned the markers, and the third medal tee looked as though it might follow it".

Council had to take urgent action and George Carlisle, a civil engineer member experienced in this field, proposed an echelon of railway sleepers with gaps of about three inches between each to act as a breaker and to allow shingle to be trapped behind by the receding undertow.

3000 sleepers

For two years the green staff, by hand and shovel, dug a trench along the foreshore 4'6" deep and about 2'6" wide. Two lines of sleepers were inserted in the trench so that half their 9' length was embedded into the foreshore with the remaining 4'6" projecting about the beach level. This work was interrupted by tides, weather and other greenkeeping priorities but by 1963 the stockade was complete from the lane between the Mourne and the hotel to a point 1,100 yards northward — a fair distance north of the then vulnerable area along the 3rd hole.

It was a massive task. More than 3000 sleepers were placed in 431 man days, but it proved effective. In more recent years an outer similar line was erected at spots damaged by the elements and by vandalism but constant vigilance is needed, and their maintenance is vital and continuous.

The British Ladies Open Amateur Championship returned in 1963 for the seventh time. The links were in splendid condition for this important match play event which included international challengers from America, Australia, France, Germany and Sweden. One was the tall and athletic American, Joanne Gunderson, then 24, who had already won the American Ladies Amateur Open three times. Her compact three-quarter swing generated an impressive power and she confided that when at home she often played with three men and from the same tee. "I like to drive first, then all the men press". She was, however, beaten 3 and 2 in the quarter final by Mlle. Claudine Cros of France, probably because of her inexperience in the fierce wind.

"I like to drive first then all the men press".

The weather, glorious during practice, had deteriorated into a raging gale that on the penultimate day snapped the heavy cross-arm of the Club flagstaff. Nevertheless, there was quality golf. The 36 hole final was between Philomena Garvey of Ireland and Brigette Varangot of France who contracted tonsillitis the night before and was advised not to play. She was not to be denied, however, and, after injections, courageously came to the first tee the next morning, but looking distinctly wan. The drug must have been effective for she won an absorbing final by 3 and 1 and became the third Frenchwoman to win this championship in the last four times it was played at Newcastle.

John Gray, Captain of the Club, presenting Brigitte Varangot of France with the 1963 British Ladies Championship Trophy.

1964 saw a return of the Irish Close Championship, with two rounds of qualifying stroke play to produce 64 players for the match play stages. Joe Carr took 81 in his first round and such was his impact on the game at that time that those on whose shoulders the success of the championship lay viewed his performance with no little dismay. However, the confident Carr said "Don't worry — I'll be there tomorrow night". And so he was, adding a 72 to qualify comfortably.

W. J. J. Ferguson. *J. B. Carr.*

The match play stages produced some excellent and exciting golf, notably an absorbing semi-final battle between Carr and W. J. J. Ferguson of Malone and Royal County Down. Carr had been two up, but Ferguson squared at the tenth and went one up with an albatross at the twelfth. He still held this lead at the 16th when Carr announced to the referee that the ball had moved as he was addressing it and he was penalising himself a shot. Nevertheless, he chipped splendidly for his half and at the seventeenth Ferguson maintained his one hole lead somewhat fortuitously by going in off Carr's ball to square the hole. On the eighteenth Ferguson missed what he himself would have regarded as a holeable putt and the match went to a tie hole, where he sliced his tee shot into shingle on the beach. The penalty thus incurred gave Carr the match and clearance of his major hurdle in a championship which he went on to win the next day, for the fourth time, with a 6 and 5 victory over Alan McDade of Bangor.

A "Character" and the Curtis Ladies

In the late 1950s Council's attention turned again to the inadequacy of the Club buildings, and a special committee was formed to consider what developments were needed and how these should be funded. Various alternatives were considered and, in 1964, a special meeting was called at which the committee chairman, John Gray, made a strong case for modernisation on the grounds that all those who had enjoyed the facilities handed down by a previous generation should consider and provide for the next. He and his committee felt that although the plan before them was too costly it was one which was correct in principle and on which changes could be based.

New looks

After much discussion the meeting agreed to provide capital by doubling subscriptions from 10 to 20 guineas. While the membership acknowledged the need for change Gray sensed some unease and wisely called a further meeting to present modified plans. In March 1965 an amended scheme altered the entire first floor to provide views of the mountains, links and sea from a new bar, and a modernised kitchen adjoined a new, enlarged dining room where the old bar had been. New locker rooms, washing facilities, and a complete new block housing professional, visitors changing facilities and other ancillary offices were included in an ambitious £60,000 scheme which was accepted by the members as a necessary and far sighted development. John Gray had guided the plans through with tact and sensitivity.

The Club always moves at a decorous pace, and in 1937 a heart-rending plea had been made on behalf of 14 "senile members" regarding the mound beside the ninth green which obscured their view of it from the Clubhouse.

"Some elderly members are now unable to play a full round but are so attached to the Club that they appear daily in the reading room. Unhappily they are confronted with the mound, the removal of which would provide an exhilaration to prolong their lives. Request that Captain and Council give this matter their consideration, as for these members time is flying."

Council rejected this cri de coeur and, despite almost endless discussions it took 30 years for them to change their minds. Their reluctance was due primarily to the length of time they felt the green staff would need to complete the work, thereby interfering with essential course maintenance. Eventually the admirable Willie Smyth, Honorary Secretary and convenor of the Green Committee, was given permission to remove it, working with his own man, tractor and trailer. This stout retainer travelled daily from Banbridge — no small distance — and Council arranged for the staff to feed him. He is said to have much enjoyed his work.

"not without relief" That year saw the long standing link with the railway ended. Up to then the Ulster Transport Authority had paid an annual fee of £100, an arrangement initiated in 1904 with the old Belfast and County Down Railway, in return for which hotel visitors enjoyed preferential green fees. It had been agreed that this sum should be increased, but the U.T.A. sold the Slieve Donard Hotel to Grand Metropolitan and the arrangement ended ("not without relief") by mutual agreement. Thus concluded close ties between the Club and the railways. Many great British courses and hotels had had their initial impetus from the growth of railways and the Club had been no exception.

In that summer's glorious weather "Shell's Wonderful World of Golf" filmed Christy O'Connor of Royal Dublin and Don January from America who won with a 68 against O'Connor's 72. The event's advance publicity attracted 5,000 spectators but it was recorded in some dismay that the £1 car parking fee produced only £39. Nevertheless it was an entertaining event to which Jimmy Demaret and Joe Carr had been invited to act as commentator and referee.

Over the years great "characters" abounded. In 1967 Jack Harvey, surely one of the most impressive, died. He was known far beyond his native heath,

Joe Carr and Jimmy Demaret

and Arthur Jones recalled that before he left Frilford Heath to take up his appointment as Secretary of the Club he was told "You will meet a man called Jack Harvey". They became firm friends and Jones later reflected that he was probably the greatest character he had ever met, a not inconsiderable compliment from a man of such discernment. Harvey was an engaging personality and adept at many sports, notably Irish international hockey, where his great skill was alleged to have brought about changes in the rules of the game. A fine fisherman and enthusiastic gambler, he had a great love of good company, a propensity for hospitality and a fund of stories, many told against himself. With it all he was a man of great kindness, rarely missing his daily visit to the Club, and when he died, some little time after retiring as a delightfully unpredictable Secretary of Down County Council, two members actually resigned because they would no longer be able to enjoy his company. Stories about him are legion, and one small incident is worth recording. Giving rein to his penchant for embellishment, he pronounced one Saturday morning that he had received a telegram from the owner of a certain horse indicating that it would win. Caddies mounted their bicycles for the local bookmakers and the members' telephone was besieged, but a more cautious soul consulted the "Belfast Newsletter" to learn that the owner was listed, simply, as The Queen.

Horse laugh

Jack Harvey.

A confidential inquiry in 1964 led to an official request early the following year to host the 1968 Curtis Cup. It was to be the first occasion on which a fullscale international match between America and British teams would take place in Ireland and Council readily accepted this most generous of compliments. It was immediately apparent that major organisation would be required for the Club agreed to underwrite the event in conjunction with the L.G.U. One leading golf writer started his concluding article:

> *"The Americans, as expected, go home with the Curtis Cup but they all want to return to Royal County Down whose members stage-managed this golf spectacular with the flawless expertise of a group of Hollywood producers."*

The organisation was meticulous, and full of thought and effort. The regulations for the golf itself were naturally under the control of the Ladies Golfing Union but the Club had to organise all other aspects

The sandhills North of the 3rd green.

Playing the 2nd shot to the dog-leg 13th.

British Isles Team

Miss A. Irvin, Miss V. Saunders, Mrs. M. Pickard, Miss B. A. Jackson, Mrs. I. C. Robertson, Miss P. Tredinnick.
Miss D. Oxley, Miss P. Roberts, Mrs. S. M. Bolton (Captain), Mrs. N. Howard.

American Team

Miss R. Albers, Miss M. L. Dill, Miss P. Conley, Miss S. Hamlin
Miss P. Preuss, Mrs. D. Welts, Mrs. Robert Monsted (Captain), Miss J. Ashley

which included course, clubhouse, communications, transport, press, radio and television, publicity, and accommodation. Bob Rolston's sub-committee was joined by Mrs. Jean McMullan, the Misses Daisy Ferguson and Moira Smyth and, later, by the Captain of the British Curtis Cup Team, Mrs. Zara Bolton.

An amusing note in the minutes of a meeting not long before the event and as a result of a discreet enquiry as to whether it was considered necessary to provide protection for the teams, recorded that "the experienced lady escorts being selected by the Ladies Club will make male bodyguards unnecessary".

Credit for such successful management must go to Rolston whose infectious energy and enthusiasm never flagged. The following year he accepted a very appropriate invitation to Captain the Club.

"... the experienced lady escorts will make male bodyguards unnecessary".

The match was played in mid June and in glorious weather. The British Isles started well and at the end of the first day led 4 matches to 3 with two halved, but hopes of victory were dashed the next day when they only managed one win and three halves, giving the U.S.A. an overall success by 10½ matches to 7½. Nevertheless it was a marvellous occasion, filled with happiness and good humour and Charles Adams, one of the youngest Captains of the Club to have held office, felt only fleeting disappointment in presenting the Curtis Cup to a most charming captain of the American team, Mrs. Evelyn Monsted of New Orleans. The Council had naturally, but unusually, agreed to "unaccompanied ladies" using all of the club rooms during the week and Mrs. Monsted, in accepting the trophy, and to the delight of her audience, was able to observe that her team's visit had achieved the distinction of disturbing but one Royal County Down tradition.

Many long standing friendships were created as a result of the Curtis Cup and a happy sequel occurred a few months later with the arrival of an elegant trophy from New Orleans, a joint gift from the Monsted, Poitevent, and Carrere families, all of whom had been present and who wished to mark tangibly their enjoyment of the occasion.

Council gratefully accepted the piece, and decreed that it should be named The New Orleans Trophy, to be awarded annually to the winners of the Club Mixed Foursomes.

The New Orleans Trophy

Mr. Charles Adams, Captain of the Club, presenting the Curtis Cup to Mrs. Robert Monsted, Captain of the United States Team.

A gratifying compliment to Rolston and his committee appeared shortly after the event, when the editor of a leading golf magazine wrote:

"I have absolutely no hesitation in claiming that the organisation of the Royal County Down Golf Club for the fifteenth Curtis Cup Match was the finest I have ever seen in my life".

The Misses Curtis would have been pleased.

Records, Rabbits and Re-birth

Just after the Curtis Cup a member, J. Mervyn Jamison, established a new course record while playing in the Clark Cup. From the regular medal tees his 66 equalled James Bruen's score in the first round of the 1939 Irish Championship but minor modifications to the course after the war, including the lengthening of the 15th hole by setting the green back some 60 yards, made this a new record which stood until Hugh Smyth equalled it two decades later. He was then a one handicap player, and his compact and elegant swing has changed little; nor has his handicap, making him a welcome partner and feared opponent.

Charles Adams' year of office was a happy one for the Club, marked not only by the Curtis Cup but also by an hilariously eventful cricket match. Eric Tucker, Headmaster of Rockport School and an umpire on the occasion, was the author of an amusing account of the contest which appeared the following week in a local paper.

J. M. Jamison.

GOLFERS AT CRICKET

As a result of a challenge hurled to and fro between the 19th holes of the Royal Belfast and Royal County Down Golf Clubs a match was played by two teams of eminent golfers who thought it not beneath them to exchange the wedge for the willow and take part in a game of cricket on the ground of Rockport School on Friday.

Winning the toss, the Royal County Down allowed their opponents the honour. D. McKee and Canon Eric Barber were sent in to face the attack of Madeley and Jamison. The latter, bowling down the hill, made the ball rise alarmingly at times, and on one occasion smote the representative Church body so severely that the wicket keeper and first slip were able to hear almost the whole of the Combination Service before the end of the over. However, both batsmen attacked the bowling with high morale and considerable skill and each had reached double figures before McKee was bowled by Cowdy who had replaced the sacreligious Jamison at the top end.

After three interesting overs from W. Webb which showed a nice variation of pace, flight and direction, Adams, the Newcastle skipper, had McMullan M. brilliantly caught by Webb R. for a rapid 31. McNeill, whose iron play behind the wicket had won the amazed admiration of friend

Not quite golf

and foe alike, gave the same bowler his second victim when he later stumped McMullan P. for a well hit 43. Dawson Moreland, the Craigavad captain, whose score was 1 over 5's after 4 overs, was out to another good catch by Webb R. off Adams. Bradley D. and Parsons T. were still in single figures but undefeated when Moreland declared at 172 for 6.

Scorning the use of either the heavy or the light roller, Adams sent in Madeley and Cowdy B. to open for Newcastle.

The old Inniskillen Dragoon, however, soon showed that he had lost none of the skill which had made the name of Cowdy terror of the land among the Irish Prep. Schools in the 1930s. Driving freely allround the wicket with an occasional 8 iron shot over mid-on, he treated all bowlers with superb contempt.

Fine catches by McMullan M. off Hannon and by Hannon off Litster accounted for the two younger members of the Webb family. J. S. Pollock scored 16 in his old familiar style before being caught one-handed by Hannon on the boundary. Webb W. ran twelve majestic singles and hit four fours and a two in his innings of 30 and was finally out to a McMullan catch off Lowry.

Cowdy, in spite of some nasty out-swingers from Parsons bowling up the hill, had reached his fifty and seemed set for the hundred. With his total at 60, however, a full-blooded drive off Moreland was most competently taken by Parsons now resting at mid-off. Harry McCaw paid a brief visit to the crease but was out to a good catch by wicket keeper Bradley D. off Moreland.

D. McKee, who had spent most of the time ferreting about in the rough in search of the occasional "lost ball" came on at the bottom end to bowl Jamison with a ball which the batsman later described as a "humdinger" and the bowler himself as "one which went with me arm."

At 8.15 p.m. Adams and McNeill, who played with the straightest of bats while throwing out hints about his inability to see the Umpire at the bowler's end, found themselves requiring about 50 runs to win with two wickets in hand. Such was his confidence that Adams exercised his option to take an extra 15 minutes play. At the end of this period McNeill retired, hurt by the refusal of the Umpires to accept his hints about the light, in favour of Adams junior, another two overs being decreed to allow the last batsman who had already fielded sub for Craigavad to have his chance for revenge on the bowlers. This he seized with both hands, clouting Moreland to the boundary for four and making his panting parent run a couple of short singles. Off the last ball of the match he would have scored another boundary had his shot not been intercepted by the square leg Umpire who just failed to bring off a smart catch. The match thus ended in a draw.

1969 began with the deferment of a decision to create a practice ground. A golf architect had been engaged to make recommendations but his solution would have meant the loss of the 1st and 18th holes on No. 2 course. With the demands of modern golf it was an ongoing problem.

The same year marked the retirement of Caddie Master Tommy Russell who had worked for the Club since leaving the army in 1919. An engaging and often crusty character he was held in great affection by the members, and a

Tommy Russell.

The Amateur

presentation to him in the bar on Saturday, May 1, marked 50 years to the day from he first reported for duty.

The following year the Club hosted the Amateur Championship, the third time it had been held in Ireland since the war. The Royal and Ancient had made the request some two years previously and in the intervening period much ground work had been done. As with the Curtis Cup, comprehensive organisation was needed and Bob Rolston again chaired the organising committee. The R. & A. shouldered the financial responsibility and some administrative work but they were satisfied that Rolston's committee was competent to handle much of the organisation which would have been difficult to deal with from St. Andrews.

The event was played in almost tropical weather and was an outstanding success. As with the Curtis Cup, Gallahers provided generous financial help, as did the Northern Ireland Tourist Board, which allowed the Club to provide a high quality tented village and hospitality to many visitors throughout the world of golf. As always, the members of the Royal County Down, the Ladies, and Mourne Clubs were supportive of the committee's efforts leading up to the Championship, and although many would have regarded it as sacreligious on a links, they accepted with equanimity the decree that

Michael Bonallack, winner of the Amateur Championship.

during the previous winter no trolleys should be brought to the course and that all fairway shots should be played off peg tees. Thus the links were in superb order.

Entries were limited to 256 but this was exceeded easily and the last places were filled by balloting the 3-handicappers. The early rounds saw much excellent golf from an international field and, as the week progressed, the sun-baked fairways became harder and faster, testing the skill of all who survived. Friday evening saw the promise of a great 36-hole final the next day. The holder, M. F. Bonallack, was set to attempt his hat trick of wins and his fifth Amateur victory, an achievement unequalled since the great John Ball won his fifth in 1899. His opponent was William Hyndman III of the U.S.A., a repeat of the same final at Hoylake the previous year.

Hyndman had had a somewhat wearying passage for in his three earlier rounds he had been taken beyond the 18th and, during the Championship itself, had played 25 more holes than Bonallack who had not gone past the 17th at any stage. So on Saturday morning Hyndman, then 54 years of age, set out to emulate the 1933 winner, the Hon. Michael Scott, as the oldest holder of the Amateur Championship.

He played well until the short 10th where a terrifyingly perfect shank almost did for the Past Captain, standing in the heather some 30 yards away and almost at right angles to the intended line of flight. Nothing daunted, he almost holed his second tee shot and completed the next seven holes in five under par. He lost the 18th, but it speaks volumes for Bonallack's golf that Hyndman only went into lunch one up. That was really the end, for the heat and hard ground had taken their toll and he set out after lunch with a blistered foot. Bonallack squared the match at the 19th with a birdie and went one up at the 20th with another. The rest of the game was a relentless and merciless display of golf by the holder who in the end retained his title by 8 and 7.

Bill Hyndman, having just missed a putt of tantalising length.

R. & A.   Both the R. & A. and the international Press were gratifyingly warm in their praise, and the week heralded many close friendships between St. Andrews and Royal County Down. As at the time of the Curtis Cup

The Club Captain, Harry McCaw, presenting Michael Bonallack with the Amateur Championship Trophy.

with Charles Adams, the Club had again honoured one of their younger members, Harry McCaw, with the Captaincy during a major event, and not long afterwards he was invited to allow his name to go forward for membership of the R. & A. In accepting this compliment, he followed Charles Adams, elected some years previously, into membership of that great golfing institution which today has close links with the Club. A number of R. & A. members are now members of Royal County Down, among them four Past Captains; similarly, some Newcastle members have close ties with St. Andrews, and C. H. Adams, J. G. McErvel, W. J. J. Fergson and McCaw have all served on R. & A. Committees (the last-named being the only golfer from Ireland to have been honoured with a seat on their General Committee — B.H.)

The "troubles" The last two decades in Northern Ireland have been bedevilled by political turmoil and violence outside this history. While it would be plain silly to pretend that there have been no effects upon the Club and Members, despite everything development continued and a widely diverse membership retained their traditional cameraderie. Naturally this extended to other clubs and, apart from the cancelled Home Internationals and two incidents, one of which could have been tragic, the Club maintained steady progress.

Costs continued to be a major concern for decimalisation in 1969 started the now all too familiar inflationary process. Conscious of the ever-increasing demands upon the courses, Council asked Harry McCaw to chair a long term course planning committee during his Captaincy. This was not new thinking but a revival of similar attempts

Gerald Annesley — Grandson of the first President.

over the years to concentrate attention on future needs. The Committee reconsidered the Pennink report for the upgrading of No. 2 Course but concluded that it would be too costly, although it made recommendations on sea defences, irrigation, tree planting and other relevant matters, including the purchase for £450 of all available portions of the old railway line bordering its property. The question of a practice ground was again deferred and did not re-emerge until 1977 when Council decided to level an area formed by the west side of the car park and first teeing area on the No. 2 Course, at that time perched on a sandhill near what was later to become Merrion Avenue. It was a controversial decision and, although it provided much needed but limited practice facilties, many still look back with affection to the long staircase of railway sleepers leading to the back tee from which many a ball was nosed sharply into the bordering whins.

During W. H. Webb's Captaincy the following year, the Ulster Youths Championship produced a notable final between Stephen Dijon of Royal Portrush and Perry Malone of Belvoir Park. In a final lasting two and a half hours, Malone holed the last nine in 32 shots to win by one hole, eliciting a compliment during the Captain's presentation that he had seen no finer golf during the previous year's Amateur Championship.

The following year the Irish Close returned to Newcastle, Kenneth Stevenson of Banbridge beating T. B. C. Hoey of Shandon Park by 2 and 1 in the final. In the championship's early stages, one senior member of the Club, on being asked to assess Stevenson's chances, rated them at 100-1 against. The odds were accepted at once by another equally experienced member (who lived not 100 miles from Banbridge Golf Club). It is understood that the proceeds were disbursed in hospitality that same evening in both Newcastle and Banbridge.

In 1973 John McCavery, a man of few words but great knowledge and experience, resigned as head greenkeeper and the Members paid tangible tribute to his 52 years of dedicated care of the course for there was little he did not understand, sometimes by instinct, about the links, and his work with Wilson Smyth on the completion, over a period of time, of H. S. Colt's recommendations, are a fitting reminder of his

"... were multiplying rapidly again ..."

talents. Walter Beattie, his able successor, came from Fortwilliam.

Myxomatosis had cleared the course of rabbits in the 1950's but they were multiplying rapidly again by the 1970s and appeared to have gained partial immunity, for although a new strain had removed them entirely from land not five miles away, it had no effect whatever at the Club. Various methods of control were tried with little success and the Secretary, Arthur Jones, devised a distinctly dubious method of gassing using the tractor's exhaust pipe. Council felt unable to disagree with his assertion that this attack had been moderately successful but the problem still remains, varying in its degree of severity. A 1700 yard rabbit fence was erected along the western boundary to link up with an existing one on the North side but, although this helped, damage continued and in the 1980s a professional rabbit catcher was employed who in one season disposed of 1768 rabbits and snared two members of the Mourne Golf Club.

Arthur C. Jones, Secretary of the Club from 1957 until 1976.

It was in 1976 that Gerald Annesley, grandson of the first President, revitalised the family's close connections with the Club when he accepted the Captaincy, and Arthur Jones retired as Secretary. During his nineteen years of office the Club never faltered and the membership was saddened by his decision although mindful of his great contribution. His affection for the Club, and for what he called "my members", remained until his death in Newcastle in 1981.

In 1977 Willie Smyth was succeeded as Honorary Secretary by Harry McCaw. His contribution to the Club had been a significant one. Modest and unassuming, a skilful golfer and expert shot, his retirement marked some 40 years in which he and his father had successively kept their firm and guiding fingers on the pulse of the Club.

Willie Smyth, son of Wilson Smyth, and Honorary Secretary for 21 years.

Over the years the Suggestion Book has been a rich reminder of bright moments. During the mid-70s the

House Committee redecorated the dining room, the new scheme receiving warm acceptance by some and an equally cool reaction from others. Shortly after it was completed a Member wrote:— *"The House Committee should resign en masse except for those who could prove they were in no way responsible for the decor in the dining room"*. The Secretary replied that the House Committee were *"as innocent and white as the driven snow"*. Which oblique answer prompted an addendum from an eminent surgeon suggesting that *"the House Committee, and indeed all the Members of Council, might be congratulated on setting such a good example by preserving their bonhomie in the sombre surroundings which now enclose us"*.

In 1979 the first of two attacks upon the Club caused minor fire damage but it was the forerunner of a second more serious one in 1981. A Saturday Council meeting had just started when a car bomb exploded at the gate into the garden. No warning was given and the west side of the Clubhouse was extensively damaged. Flames engulfed the bomb vehicle and there was substantial damage to members' cars. (Miraculously the only injury was sustained by the caddie master, Jimmy Williamson who sustained cuts and, sadly, died some months later of a heart attack.) Council formed a labour squad to remove glass and debris and by noon "The Hat" (the Club's traditional name for a draw for Saturday games which had originated in the distant past when slips of paper were shuffled in a red top hat on the golfers' train) was declared open and lunch was served as usual. In the bar the stout-hearted and imperturbable steward, Willie Magee, was seen to perspire gently and laconically remark that things seemed "slightly busier than normal Sir", and the Club flag, which had been flying at half mast in memory of a recently deceased member, was raised to the top of the yardarm.

"The stout-hearted and imperturbable club steward, Willie Magee".

G.U.I. The Club has, through its membership, always been a major contributor to sport in Ireland and 1980 saw Michael McAuley as President of the Golfing Union of Ireland and Stuart Pollock President of the Irish Cricket Union. Pollock, a former Captain of the Club and of the Gentlemen of Ireland was regarded by many as one of the finest fielders ever to represent his country. In 1976 the G.U.I. Presidency was held by J. G. McErvel, and in 1984 and 1988 by W. J. J. Ferguson and B. T. Crymble.

John Boston.

Sadly, no brilliant golfing youngsters have emerged recently, but members of riper years have continued to display flair and enthusiasm. John Boston, perhaps the greatest aficionado of all, and certainly the only member known to have travelled from Belfast to Newcastle to practise on Christmas Day, brought honour to the Club by winning the Irish Seniors Championship in 1984 and 1985 and only just failing to win the British Seniors that same year by one shot. Not to be outdone the Club's genial and respected Professional, Ernie Jones, won the British Seniors Professional Championship in 1984 and the Irish in 1986.

In the early part of the 1987 golfing season a *cri de coeur* reached the Secretary's desk from that same eminent surgeon who had commented upon the dining room decor 10 years earlier. It is worth recording for it epitomises the sense of fun that ought always to remain among all who play the greatest of amateur games:

"My dear Richard,
I am sure that you will be deeply shocked, as I am, to learn that I am now in my seventyninth year.

I have had a handicap of seventeen since I was a strapping 75, but unhappily some miscreant has lengthened all the fairways and contrived to make the stairs much steeper. I find this a burden beyond what my failing vigour can bear. Do you think that the handicapping committee would consider that 20 or maybe 21 might enable me to enjoy the few years that remain to me; and so that I may make my way into the sunset in peace and tranquility.
Best regards,
Yours sincerely,

P.S. Forgive the tearstains; my sad story is more than I can bear."

"... that same eminent surgeon"
— David Craig.

And so the first 100 years began moving to a close and thoughts turned to the Centenary. Apart from celebrations to mark the occasion in 1989 Council felt it appropriate to look ahead once more and provide the Club with enhanced facilities. A leading agronomist's advice had been accepted and major expenditure had taken place on course and

An aerial view of both courses taken in 1988.

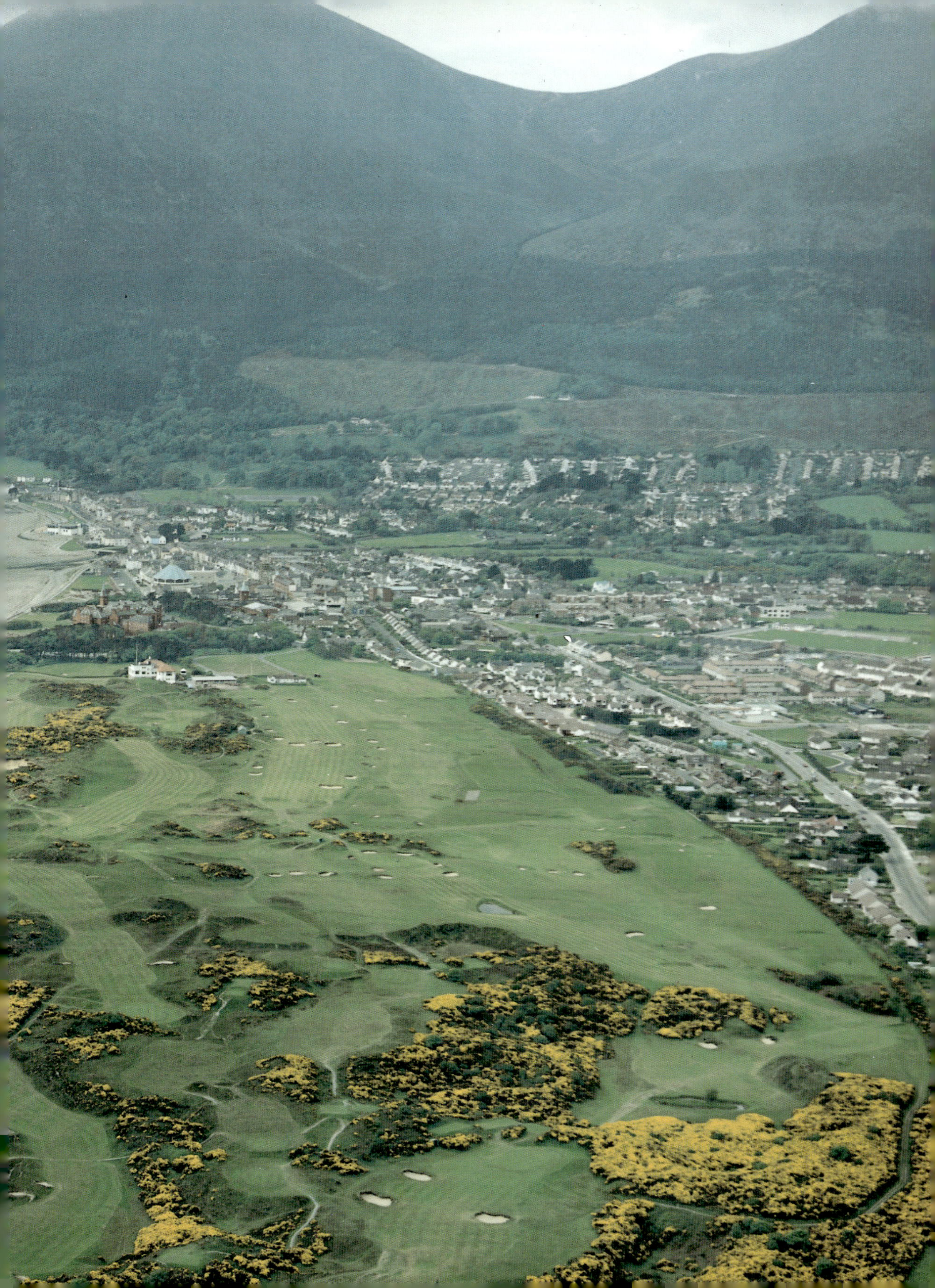

equipment but the Club, as ever, was high in world esteem and Council felt that facilities were still inadequate for the increasing number of overseas golfing vistors. The membership responded most generously to an appeal for a fine extension on the North side in keeping with the rest of the building and with a major interior refurbishment, all of which was completed in 1988, the Club was able to look ahead with confidence towards a second century.

Looking back over all that has happened in a hundred years of golf at Newcastle it is more often the memories and friendships, the intangible things, that make Royal County Down the rather special institution that it is. To be a member, and to play on a links set among such beauty, is privilege of high order.

Perhaps, though, the last words should be those of Willie Haughton and Huw Wallace, great contributors to the life of the Club 60 years ago, and whose sense of fun encapsulated for all time the frustrations, the hopes, and the laughter in the most absorbing game of all:—

"It is a matter of general comment that we British, who once were supreme in all manner of sport, are nowadays unable to hold our own with the foreigners. Especially is this so in the realm of golf, the game of all others at which we fancied ourselves. The reason for this seems to be that we approach it in a spirit of thoughtless levity, while other nations regard it as a matter of scientific study.

The following verses contain a suggestion towards a more serious and methodical attitude on the part of some of our members, and are inscribed with all due respect to my friend P.T.C. (Professor P. T. Crymble) who, at the beginning of a month's golfing last August (1925), made the following memorable resolution:—

"Henceforth I will take this game seriously"

1. *Of modern thought's torrential flow*
   That finds in print it's fitting ventage,
   The lucubrations of the Pro
   Monopolise a large percentage;
      Each day some Harry, George, or Bill
      Lays down the cleek to grab the quill.

2. *The raison d'etre of the wrist,*
   The knees, the interlocking fingers,
   The tibia's peculiar twist —
   On themes like these his fancy lingers
      With subtleties which he's aware
      Are to the general mere caviare.

3. *Entranced we burn the midnight oil*
   To learn the secret of 'the Pivot,'
   How best to sever from the soil
   The harmless necessary divot
      And finally, that flail-like draggle
      The hall-mark of a polish'd 'waggle'.

4. *And lest perchance it happen that*
   By tedium we be afflicted
   The Pro himself is cinemat-
   ographically found depicted
      Most resolutely gazing where
      The lines 'A' 'B' form half a square.

5. So having sedulously read
   Enough didacto-prophylactics
   To put an end to 'Swaying head'
   or socketting, or faulty tactics
       How eagerly we seize the Club
       And face the Ball! Ay there's the rub!

6. O small malign hypnotic thing
   Reposing under one's proboscis
   Satanically power'd to bring
   A palsy o'er the psychic process!
       Tips that I'd stored with miser care
       Have vanish'd wrackless into air!

7. But wise provision I have made,
   In future there 'll be no debâcle
   I'll take the works of Duncan, Braid,
   And Vardon with my usual tackle
       Two mentor-caddies loud shall read
       Before each shot the texts I need.

8. Then surely one should not forget
   The benefits of Modern Science
   On Camera and Dynamo
   Implicitly I place reliance
       To reproduce my every Round.
       (If further Caddies can be found.)

9. Thus after dinner in my chair
   My faults (if any) criticising,
   I'll gather from the Movies where
   My methods chance to need revising —
       Some years of simple practice thus
       D.V. will make my minus plus.

                        W.B.H.

Harry McCaw and Brum Henderson © 1988

CAPTAINS OF THE CLUB

1889/90	A. Lowry-Corry	1949	C. F. F. Davies, C.B.E.
1891	Lord Arthur Hill	1950	W. R. Knox
1892	Henry Gregg	1951	I. H. McCaw, M.D.
1893	Major R. H. Wallace	1952	N. B. G. Harvey
1894	Thomas Dickson	1953	J. C. Robb, M.D.
1895/96	George Combe	1954	H. L. Hardy Greer, F.R.C.S.
1897	R. Magill	191955	J. D. Ferguson, O.B.E.
1898/99	F. Hoey	1956	R. W. Hutchinson
1900	Colonel Cutbill	1957	Sir Frank Montgomery, M.C.
1901	G. S. Clark	1958	J. A. Barr
1902/03	E. Young	1959	Wm. Smyth
1904	G. Combe	1960	R. L. Hamilton
1905	F. F. Figgis	1961	A. E. Knight
1906	J. S. Reade	1962	G. E. Cameron
1907	F. L. Heyn	1963	J. M. Gray M.B.E.
1908	Earl of Shaftesbury	1964	W. Brice Smyth
1909/10	Earl Annesley	1965	W. A. McNeill
1911	Col. R. H. Wallace, C.B.	1966	A. C. H. Houston
1912	H. V. Coates	1967	C. W. Kidd, O.B.E., M.D., F.R.C.P.
1913/14	W. H. K. Lowry	1968	C. H. Adams
1915/16	Fred H. Rogers	1969	R. D. Rolston
1917/18	Wm. McMullan	1970	I. H. McCaw
1919/20	R. J. Johnstone, F.R.C.S.	1971	W. H. Webb
1921/22	D. W. Smyth, D.L.	1972	D. H. Craig, F.R.C.S.
1923	F. Hoey	1973	A. W. S. Adams
1924	A. T. Herdman	1974	M. G. Nelson, M.D., F.R.C.S.
1925	Stanley Ferguson	1975	J. S. Pollock
1926/27	H. G. B. Ellis	1976	G. F. Annesley
1928	J. E. Wilson	1977	G. B. Purce
1929/30	Wm. Barnett	1978	G. B. Hobart
1931	D. W. Smyth, D.L.	1979	H. B. Mercer O.B.E.
1932/33	A. Fullerton, C.B., C.M.G.	1980	J. B. A. Stafford
1934	M. Gordon	1981	J. G. McErvel
1935/36	His Honour Judge Thompson, K.C.	1982	C. W. Jenkins
1937/38	P. T. Crymble, F.R.C.S.	1983	W. A. Brown
1939/42	J. Sydney Rogers	1984	T. K. Pedlow
1943/44	James A. Craig	1985	R. Barnett
1945	D. W. Smyth, D.L.	1986	J. C. Morton
1946	S. C. Ferguson	1987	J. B. Haldane
1947	S. T. Irwin, F.R.C.S.	1988	I. W. L. Webb
1948	F. M. R. Byers	1989	I. H. McCaw

HONORARY SECRETARIES

1889	G. L. Baillie and Colonel Ross
1890 and 1891	Ernest Young and R. H. Wallace
1892 to 1896	Robert Magill
1897 to 1899	Colonel H. D. Cutbill
1900 and 1901	Fred Hoey
1902 and 1903	W. J. MacGeagh
1904 to 1922	Fred Hoey
1923 to 1934	F. H. Rogers
1935 and 1936	B. C. Quarry
1936 to 1953	D. W. Smyth
1953 to 1956	S. C. Ferguson
1956 to 1977	William Smyth
1977 –	I. H. McCaw

CHAMPIONSHIPS HELD AT NEWCASTLE

IRISH OPEN AMATEUR CHAMPIONSHIP

	Winners	Runners-up
1893	J. Ball, jun. (Royal Liverpool)	L. S. Anderson (N. Berwick)
1896	W. B. Taylor (Carlton)	D. Anderson (Panmure)
1900	H. H. Hilton (Royal Liverpool)	S. H. Fry (Royal Mid-Surrey)
1904	J. S. Worthington (Royal Mid-Surrey)	J. F. Mitchell (Royal Musselburgh)
1908	J. F. Mitchell (Royal Musselburgh)	H. M. Cairnes (Portmarnock)
1912	G. Lockhart (Prestwick St. Nicholas)	P. G. Jenkins (Troon)
1921	D. W. Smyth (Royal Co. Down)	J. Gorry (Kildare)
1923	G. N. C. Martin (Royal Portrush)	C. O. Hezlet (Royal Portrush)
1927	R. M. McConnell (Royal Portrush)	D. E. B. Soulby (Fairhaven)
1931	E. A. McRuvie (Leven Thistle)	D. E. B. Soulby (Fortwilliam)
1933	J. McLean (Hayston)	E. W. Fiddian (Stourbridge)
1938	J. Bruen, jun. (Cork)	J. R. Mahon (Co. Sligo)
1948	C. Ewing (Co. Sligo)	J. B. Carr (Sutton)
1955	J. F. Fitzgibbon (Cork)	J. W. Hulme (Warrenpoint)
1959	J. Duncan (Shandon Park)	A. G. Gordon (Troon St. Meddans)

IRISH CLOSE AMATEUR CHAMPIONSHIP

	Winners	Runners-up
1894	R. Magill (Co. Down)	T. Dickson (Co. Down)
1897	H. E. Reade (Royal Belfast)	W. H. Webb (Royal Portrush)
1901	W. H. Boyd (Portmarnock)	H. E. Reade (Royal Belfast)
1905	F. B. Newett (Malone)	B. O'Brien (Malone)
1909	A. H. Patterson (Dublin University)	E. F. Spiller (Malone)
1924	J. D. MacCormack (Hermitage)	D. E. B. Soulby (Portmarnock)
1964	J. B. Carr (Sutton)	A. McDade (Bangor)
1972	K. Stevenson (Banbridge)	T. B. C. Hoey (Shandon Park)
1980	R. Rafferty (Warrenpoint)	M. J. Bannon (Belvoir Park)

OPEN CHAMPIONSHIP OF IRELAND

	Winners	Runners-up
1928	E. R. Whitcombe (288)	A. Compston (292)
1935	E. R. Whitcombe (after tie, 292)	R. A. Whitcombe (292)
1939	A. Lees (287)	R. A. Whitcombe (289)

IRISH PROFESSIONAL CHAMPIONSHIP

	Winners	Runners-up
1909	M. Moran (Royal Dublin)	H. Kidd (Malone)
1914	C. W. Pope (Fortwilliam)	J. O'Hare (Skerries)
1929	H. McNeill (Royal Portrush)	C. W. Pope (Fortwilliam)
1954	H. Bradshaw (Portmarnock)	C. O'Connor (Bundoran)

IRISH LADIES' CLOSE CHAMPIONSHIP

	Winners	Runners-up
1896	Miss N. Graham (Co. Down)	Miss E. Brownrigg (Royal Portrush)
1899	Miss May Hezlet (Royal Portrush)	Miss Rhona Adair (Killymoon)
1902	Miss Rhona Adair (Killymoon)	Miss M. E. Stuart (Royal Portrush)
1906	Miss May Hezlet (Royal Portrush)	Miss F. Hezlet (Royal Portrush)
1910	Miss M. Harrison (Island Malahide)	Miss Magill (Royal Co. Down)
1922	Mrs. Claude Gotto (Kingstown)	Miss M. R. Hirsch (Armagh)
1926	Miss P. Jameson (Island Malahide)	Mrs. C. H. Murland (Royal Co. Down)
1933	Miss E. Pentony (Hermitage)	Miss F. Blake (Hermitage)
1952	Miss Dorothy Foster (Balmoral)	Mrs. P. G. McCann (Tullamore)
1961	Mrs. K. McCann (Tullamore)	Miss A. Sweeney (Cushendall)

THE LADIES' BRITISH OPEN AMATEUR CHAMPIONSHIP

	Winners	Runners-up
1899	Miss May Hezlet	Miss Magill
1907	Miss May Hezlet	Miss F. Hezlet
1920	Miss Cecil Leitch	Miss M. Griffiths
1927	Mlle. S. Thion de la Chaume	Miss D. Pearson
1935	Miss W. Morgan	Miss P. Barton
1950	Vicomtesse de Saint Sauveur	Mrs. G. Valentine
1963	Mlle B. Varangot	Miss P. Garvey

THE CURTIS CUP

1968 U.S.A. 10½ Matches
Gt. Britain & Ireland 7½ matches.

THE AMATEUR CHAMPIONSHIP

Winner
1970 M. F. Bonallack (Thorpe Hall) Wm. Hyndman III (U.S.A.)

THE HOME INTERNATIONALS

1933 and 1957

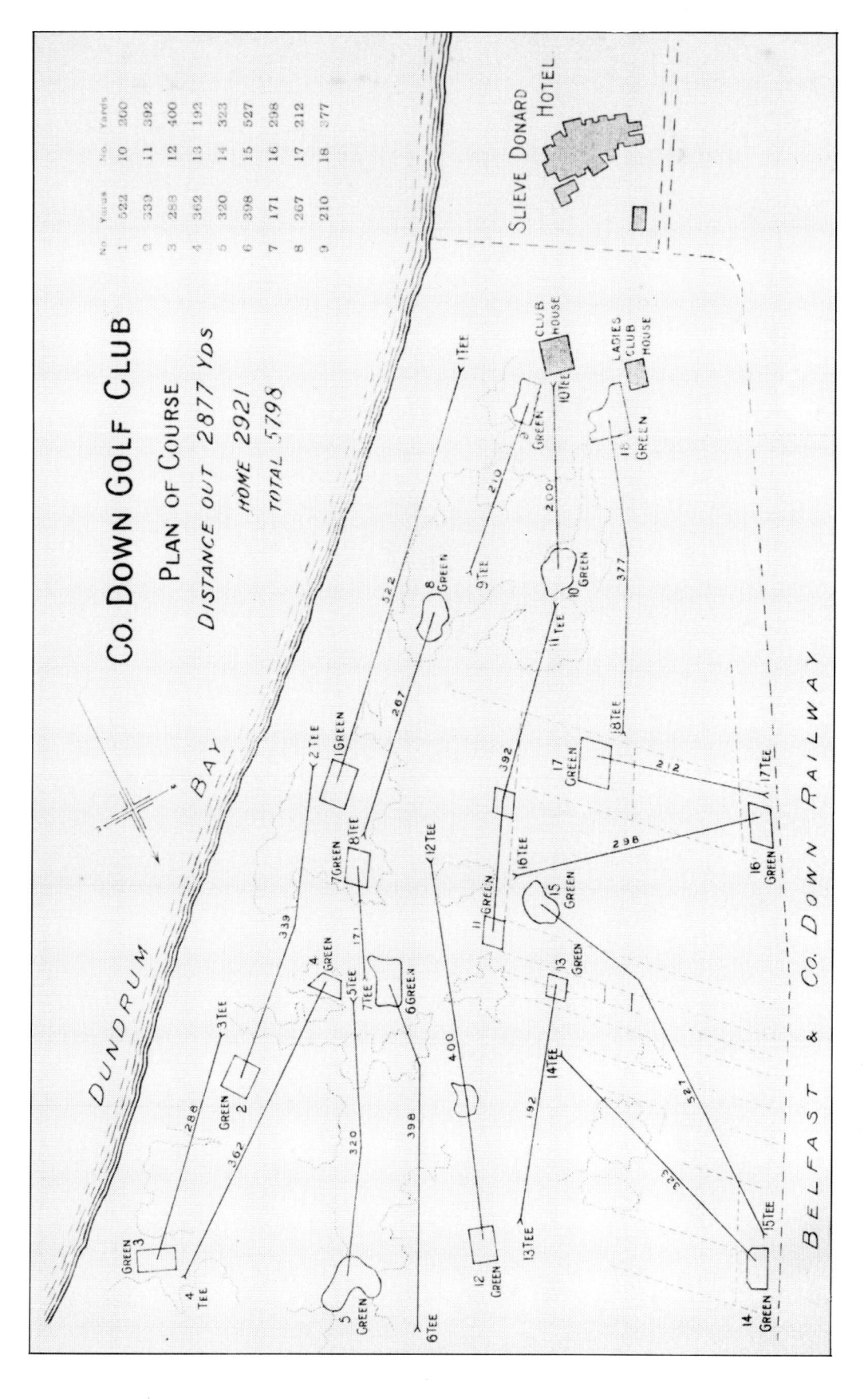

"Layout of course (circa 1900) showing major changes since the first links in 1889."

The Royal County Down Golf Club wishes to place on record their gratitude to the following Companies who expressed a wish to be associated with the Centenary and the future of golf at Newcastle:—

Aircraft Furnishing Limited	Hobart & Heron
Allied Irish Bank	Laing Markey Lyness Limited
Andrews Milling Limited	Lamont Holdings PLC
Antony Gibbs Benefit Consultants Ltd	Arthur McCann Ltd
Bank of Ireland Group	McLaughlin and Harvey PLC
W & R Barnett Ltd	Maxol Oil Limited
Bass Ireland Ltd	Menary Travel Ltd
Belleek Pottery Ltd	Brian Morton & Co
British Midland Airways	Nationwide Anglia Estate Agents
Calor Gas Northern Ireland Ltd	The "News Letter", Belfast
CIC Properties Ltd	Northern Bank Limited
Coca-Cola Bottlers (Ulster) Ltd	Northern Ireland Tourist Board
Andrew G Crawford & Co	Precision (Machine Tools) Ltd
James P Corry Holdings Ltd	Price Waterhouse
Davidson & Hardy (Laboratory Supplies) Ltd	Septembers Advertising & Marketing Ltd
Deloitte Haskins & Sells	Shell Northern Ireland
Fuel Services Northern Ireland	"Sunday News"
Gilbey's of Northern Ireland	Superlay Felts Ltd
John Graham (Dromore) Ltd	John Thompson & Sons Ltd
Greenline Services (NI) Ltd	TSB Northern Ireland PLC
Arthur Guiness Son & Company	Tyrone Brick Ltd
	Ulster Bank Group
The Haldane Shiells Group	Ulster Television PLC
Harris Marrian & Co Ltd	Universities Press (Belfast) Ltd
Hastings Hotels Group Ltd	Woolwich Equitable Building Society

COUNTY DO

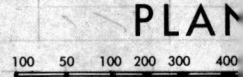

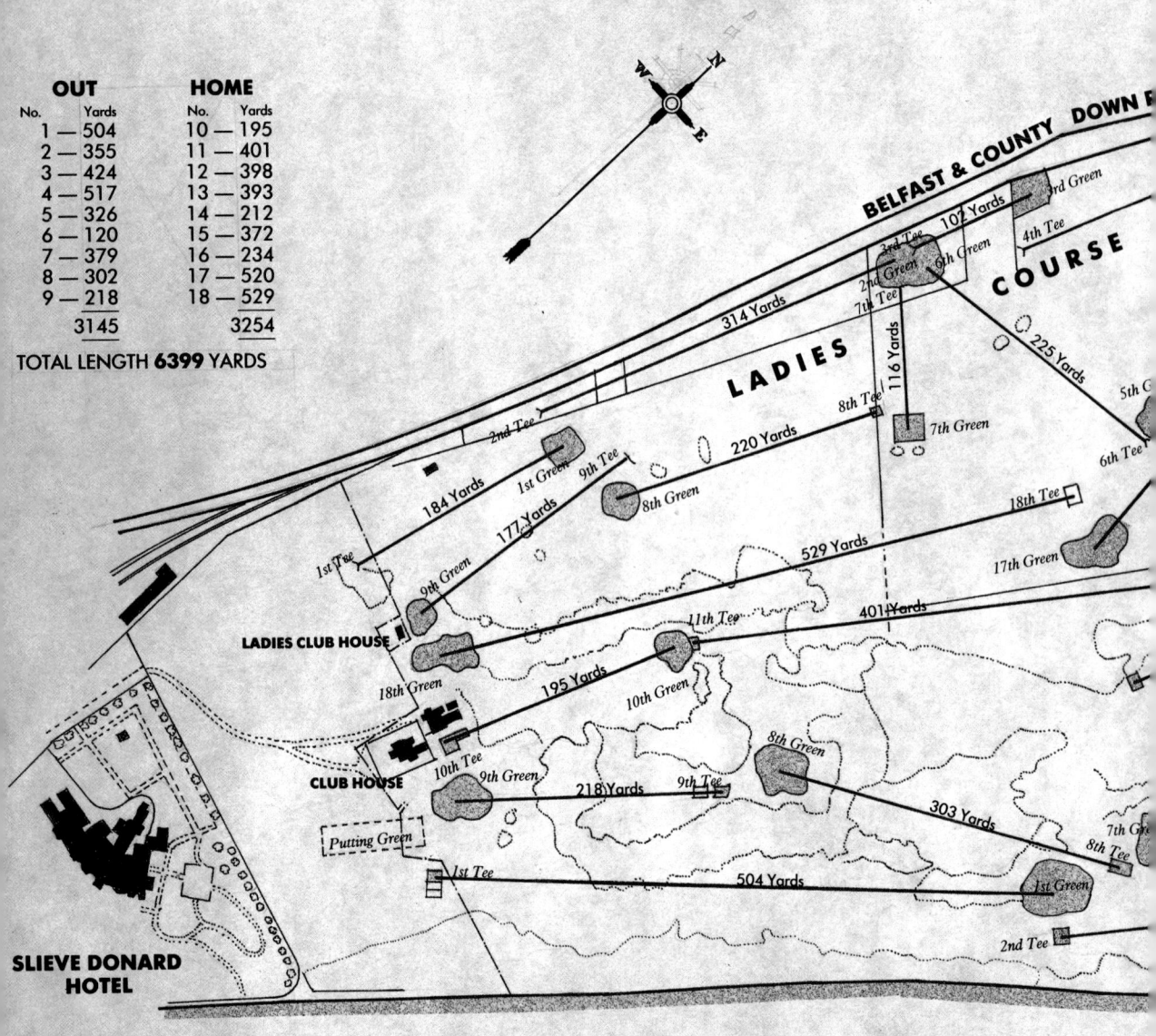

PLAN

OUT		HOME	
No.	Yards	No.	Yards
1	504	10	195
2	355	11	401
3	424	12	398
4	517	13	393
5	326	14	212
6	120	15	372
7	379	16	234
8	302	17	520
9	218	18	529
	3145		3254

TOTAL LENGTH 6399 YARDS

LADIES COURSE
1 — 184
2 — 314
3 — 112
4 — 324
5 — 326
6 — 225
7 — 116
8 — 260
9 — 177
TOTAL 2038 YARDS

SLIEVE DONARD HOTEL

LADIES CLUB HOUSE

CLUB HOUSE

DUNDRUM

BELFAST & COUNTY DOWN

LADIES COURSE